Outside the Box Performance: How to Beat Your Competitors' Brains Out

Outside the Box Performance: How to Beat Your Competitor's Brains Out. Copyright © 1996 Gary D. Zeune, CPA. All rights reserved. Printed and bound in the United States of America. No part of this book may be used or reproduced in any manner whatsoever (including mechanical or electronic storage and retrieval systems) without written permission except in the case of brief quotations embodied in critical articles or reviews. Forward one copy of any article including any work from this book to the author at:

Gary D. Zeune

285 Pinney Dr. #300

Worthington, OH 43085

ISBN 0-9643563-0-9

First Edition
10 9 8 7 6 5 4 3 2 1

Cover design by:
Bozanka Kiprovska
1740 Brice Rd. #11
Reynoldsburg, OH 43068
614-861-2795

Dedicated to Tiffany, who, by enduring my long work hours and frequent absences from home made this book possible. Tiffany is the best daughter a father could ask for.

STAY UP-TO-DATE . . . FREE

Receive Mr. Zeune's free electronic newsletter on techniques used by world-class companies to beat their competitors' brains out. Simply send an email to

GZFRAUD@BIGFOOT.COM

with the message

SUBSCRIBE PERFORMANCE.

Unsubscribe at anytime. If any questions, call Mr. Zeune at 614-885-0262 or send an email to the above address.

Foreword

Watching my consulting clients measure what drives the numbers on their financial statement is like watching a light bulb come on in a dark room. In fact, it reminds me of a story. Seems a fellow walks into a room. Half the room is brightly lit. The other half is pitch dark. His friend is on his hands and knees in the brightly lit half of the room. The fellow asks, "What are you doing?" The friend says, "I'm hunting for my contact lens." "Where did you loose it?" the fellow asks. The friend points over his shoulder to the dark half of the room. The fellow asks, "If you lost it in the dark half of the room, why are you hunting for it over here?" "Because there's more light over here," the friend says.

Isn't that like accountants who spend hours analyzing financial data, but the answer to why revenues are down isn't in the financial records; it's in the operational records. Customer satisfaction may be down because delivery times are slowing, or any one of hundreds of things that can happen. Accountants are experts at measuring. To remain indispensable, accountants must get outside their traditional frame of reference — financial statements.

If the CEO or owner had to outsource either operations or the accounting function as not critical to the company's future, which department do you think would be outsourced?

This book was a joy to write, and rewrite, and rewrite. Many sources have contributed. Although three editors have made their way through it, errors always remain undetected, and they are completely mine. If you find any, I would appreciate your sending or faxing a copy of the page with the error pointed out.

Also, please contact me with your stories of success and failures — what works, what doesn't work. Sharing your experiences will help everyone in this fight to make the accounting profession vital to your success.

Gary Zeune, CPA
285 Pinney Drive #300
Columbus, OH 43085
Phone   614-885-0262
Fax   614-885-1712
Internet gzfraud@bigfoot.com

Where Do Profits Come From?

How long do you stand in line at McDonalds before you get irritated that you don't have your food? Do you have a touch-tone phone? Think back to the last time you had to make a call using a rotary-dial phone. How long did that take? Some people say, "About a year." Do you leave your finger in the dial to make it go back around faster? Ever run a red light?

Why? What do all these things have in common? They are time sensitive. You don't want to wait. Have your customers ever been to McDonalds, or do they have touch-tone phones, or do they run red lights? Of course they have. Are your clients or customers time sensitive? What are the odds that your clients expect the same type of service from you? They do.

The basis of competition is not static, it changes every decade. In the 1970s, a world-class company was the low-cost leader. In the 1980s, customers decided that low-cost wasn't enough. So, companies responded by improving quality. The combination of price and quality is called "value." As you've seen, in the 1990s, the basis of competition is speed. What will be the basis of competition in the year 2000? My crystal ball isn't better than any one else's, but I'm putting my money on "mass customization." Sometimes called "manufacturing-to-order" or "flexibility," mass customization means companies don't make it if they don't have an order.

Don't confuse flexibility with variety. Customers don't want variety. Paradoxically, they only want the product or service the way *they* want it. In other words, customers don't want limited variety, they want infinite variety. Think back to your last trip to the grocery store. How many different cold cereals does a large store carry? Typically, more than 300. How many do you have in your house? Probably three or four. When you shop, do you evaluate each cereal? No, you don't. If you evaluate all 300, you would go into sensory overload. You buy the three or four you want and run out of the cereal section. The cereal section is an example of variety — carrying large amounts of inventory to satisfy the customer. Flexibility would be walking up to a soda size machine, punching in Kellogg, corn flakes, 20 oz. box, and it's made on the spot.

There is nothing so inefficient as making efficient that which should not be done at all.
Peter Drucker

For a few years, I had ABC Lawn Care spray my yard with a combination of fertilizer and weed control mix. The last time though, the fertilizer worked, but the weed killer didn't. I didn't pay the bill in the usual few days. George, the owner, called to find out if something was wrong. I told him my grass was growing great, but the weeds were growing even better. George replied he had a "total customer satisfaction" guarantee, and would be out in a few days to spray my lawn a second time — at no charge. I assumed George had simply forgotten to add the weed killer the first time.

A week or so later, I returned from another trip, and ABC had treated the grass again. With two fertilizer treatments in two weeks, the grass was a foot tall, but the weeds were even taller. When I still didn't pay the bill, George called a second time, demanding payment because he had fulfilled his "satisfaction guaranteed" commitment — he sprayed my yard a second time. I responded that my weeds were still growing. The light never came on for George. Like many business people, George focused on his effort (spraying) rather than the results (green grass and no weeds). Effort is easy to measure. Results are difficult to measure, but much more relevant.

Even the military gets confused. At the end of the Persian Gulf War in 1991, the military was bragging about the high

Financial statements. . . fuzzy approximations of a distant past

success rate of its "smart weapons." For example, the Air Force told Congress that the stealth fighter had an 80 percent success rate on its bombing runs. In fact, the rate was more like 40 percent. Why? The General Accounting Office found that commanders defined "success" as *launching* a bomb or missile, not hitting the target.[1] Other than counting inventory, do you think the soldiers on the ground cared how many missiles the Air Force LAUNCHED? No, they only care whether the missile took out the target.

What Business Are You In?

Write down what business you are in: _____

_____

_____

If you wrote down something like "health care," "construction," "public accounting," that's wrong. These are the things you "do," not the business you are in. So, what business are you in? The business of **solving customer problems**. It doesn't matter how good your company or firm is at "doing things." If you don't solve customer or client problems, you won't generate any revenue because customers don't have a reason to do business with you.

---

[1] "Gulf War weapons stories a pack of lies, report says," *New York Times,* as reported in *The Columbus (Ohio) Dispatch*, July 14, 1996, p. 8A.

Even if you sell hard goods, you're in the business of solving customer problems. Think about the last time you bought a car. Did you really want a car, or were you solving the problem of getting from point A to point B? What will get you into a dealer showroom that you've never been in before? Brand, model, style, but price is what initially attracts most people into the showroom the first time. After purchasing the first car at a particular dealer, what will get you to buy another one from that dealer? Overwhelmingly, most say service. So, after solving customer problems, at the next level down, everyone is in the service business.

What's the difference between these two views of the world? If, for example, you answered "health care," you are focusing on your effort, and your view is internal. If you answered "Solving customer problems," your view is external. Customers don't care how much effort you put into your work, they only care whether or not you solve their problems. Ever have an airline lose your luggage? Did you care how hard, or how many, airline employees worked at finding your luggage? Probably not. You only want your bags, and don't care how much effort it takes.

Does Quality Make a Difference?

We discussed how customers evaluate the combination of quality and price, called value, but does it make any difference to the bottom line? Definitely. According to Profit Impact of Marketing Study (PIMS), a ten-year study of nearly 1000 companies in several hundred industries by the Strategic Planning Institute, a direct relationship exists between a company's quality, market share and return on investment (ROI). The Does Quality Lead to Profits graph on page 7 depicts how much more profitable high quality companies are than the industry average.

Here is what some leading business people have to say about quality programs, people who have made the trip, and succeeded where most fail.

ROBERT GALVIN, Chairman of Executive Committee and former CEO, Motorola:

> "I don't think TQM programs are a failure. All those that have been well-managed are a great success. . ."

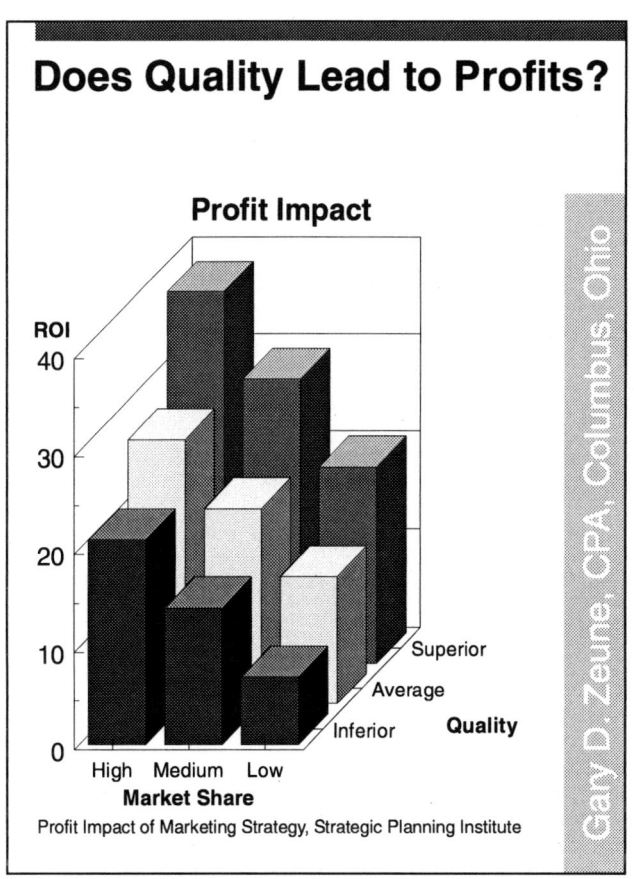

JOSEPH JURAN, quality guru:

> ". . . most frequent reason for failure is the failure of upper managers to have personal involvement"

LEWIS PLATT, Chairman, President and CEO, Hewlett-Packard:

"TQM has saved...$800 million in warranty costs during the decade."

TOM PETERS:

"...failed for three reasons.

First, TQM is a way of life, not a program. Second, [failure] to believe in the capability of front-line employee. Third, many quality programs are not customer-focused"

ROSABETH MOSS KANTOR, Harvard Business School, author of 11 books:

"Because it's mounted as a program, unconnected to business strategy, rigidly and narrowly applied, miraculous short-term transformations are expected without top management lifting a finger."

JACK WEST, President, American Society of Quality Control:

"Many look at TQM as ways to reduce defects, increase training, motivation and involvement without determining if these are important to the business. TQM must be unique to your culture and customers, and respect your history. Focus on things that add value to the customer."

CHRISTOPHER HART, President of the TQM Group, *Extraordinary Guarantees:*

"TQM is not simply a set of tools applied by teams but a radically different system . . . based on . . . prevention, management by fact, employee satisfaction and growth."

BRUCE WOOLPERT, CEO, Graniterock, 1992 Baldrige Award winner:

"TQM must be led by the management team and involve employees from the beginning."

MICHELE HUNT, Director of Federal Quality Institute:

"TQM is not a destination, it's a journey. . .constantly changing to respond to changing conditions."

JOHN CLANCEY, CEO, Sea-Land Services:

> "TQM can be threatening to employees, viewed as a method for headcount reductions. Reward and recognition are essential, and must be tied to performance, goals and objectives."

RON HEIDKE, VP and Director of Quality at Eastman Kodak:

> "Successful programs require three components: skill, knowledge and will."

DAVID GREGERSON, VP for Quality, Carrier Corporation:

> "TQM is a triangle: management leadership, employee involvement and technical systems. TQM must be linked to your business strategy and management must believe in them."

Why think outside the box?

In a CFO Magazine survey, 30 percent of CFOs considered themselves a valuable member of the management team. Yet, only 5 percent of their CEO bosses considered their CFOs a valuable member of the management team. The result? CEOs of leading edge companies are reevaluating every cost center in their companies, including support departments, like accounting. These CEO's are giving each department a choice: either be the low cost leader in providing accounting services, or provide a service that can't be obtained anywhere else (i.e., differentiate the service) to justify your price premium.

Another example, Hewlett-Packard, the electronics giant and world-class company, decided it's core competency is NOT in running warehouses. HP's core competency is building computers and printers. So, several years ago, it contracted with Roadway Express to operate its laser printer warehouse. Roadway now runs the warehouse with 140 employees, replacing 250 HP employees, which were transferred to other HP operations. Roadway's business is logistics, honed during years of over-the-road experience, a competence the HP warehouse employees didn't have. Outsourcing has reduced the cost of HP's warehouse operations by 10%.

Where will all this end? In a concept called a "company in a box." The best example to date is a small company doing $80 million a year selling the "Topsy Tail." Topsy Tail is a product sold to women with long hair. The company has only **three** employees. These three employees possess the core competencies: strategic vision, marketing and management of strategic alliances and outsourcing. All other functions are outsourced. Few existing companies will be able to emulate this structure, but some will try.

Business is Like a Ball Game

Think of business as a baseball game. If you want to know who won the game, look at the scoreboard. But, if you are the losing team and want to win the next game, you can't get better by watching the scoreboard. You have to focus on improving your batting, pitching, fielding, and catching. In business, these are called nonfinancial performance measures or operational performance measures.

In the case of McDonalds, do you think time to serve a customer is important? Of course it is. But do you find it anywhere in the financial statements? No. This is one reason the current model of financial reporting we have used the last 50 years has outlived is usefulness and is dangerously close to becoming obsolete. Current financial reporting, by its nature, is historical. It's a *lagging indicator* of performance. Is it any wonder, that if a CFO's job is to tell management what it already knows, only 5 percent of CEOs consider their CFOs valuable members of management? Another analogy: Think of your business as a bus. If the accountant is driving the bus, is the accountant looking out the windshield, or in the rear-view mirror?

So how do 21st century accountants make themselves valuable to management? By helping management measure *leading indicators*. If you don't want to be known as a "bean counter", don't just count how many beans there are, figure out where the beans came from. Determine what "drives" the numbers on the financial statements.

> **One of your most powerful weapons is to give your competitors all of your worst customers!**

On April 10th, I called a computer superstore to buy my tax software. I was put in the automatic que. Just by coincidence, the store manager picked up the call. I told him I had been on hold for about three minutes, and did he know how many calls he lost because of the long wait. He immediately said his store loses 40 percent of the calls after a three minute wait. As noted in the PHONE STATISTICS on page 18, 34 percent of first-time callers wont' call back. Their business is lost forever. Yet we don't attempt to measure this critical item — lost revenue.

So, I wondered if any other companies were aware of the effect of abandoned calls. I found a large manufacturer that had done a sophisticated study of its sales. Ninety percent of its orders are taken over the phone. Several years ago, someone asked the question, "I wonder how we're doing?" The company found out the order department was answering 85 percent of the incoming calls by the third ring. Not bad they thought.

Then someone suggested that maybe they could do better. The accountant chimed in, "We're answering 85 percent of the calls by the third ring. Why would we need to do better?" The marketing VP suggested that maybe customers demanded better service. So the company installed a "black box" to find out the "abandon rate." That is, how many customers were hanging up, abandoning their effort to purchase from the company.

The results astonished management. Ten percent of the callers were hanging up after three rings. How often does the phone ring? Don't know, even though you have a phone and it rings nonstop during business hours. About every four or five seconds in most systems. How would you like to increase your revenue ten percent by reacting ten seconds faster? Just answer on the first ring. AMP now answers 98+ percent of its calls by the third ring.

> **The significant problems we face can not be solved at the same level of thinking we were at when we created them.**
> **Albert Einstein**

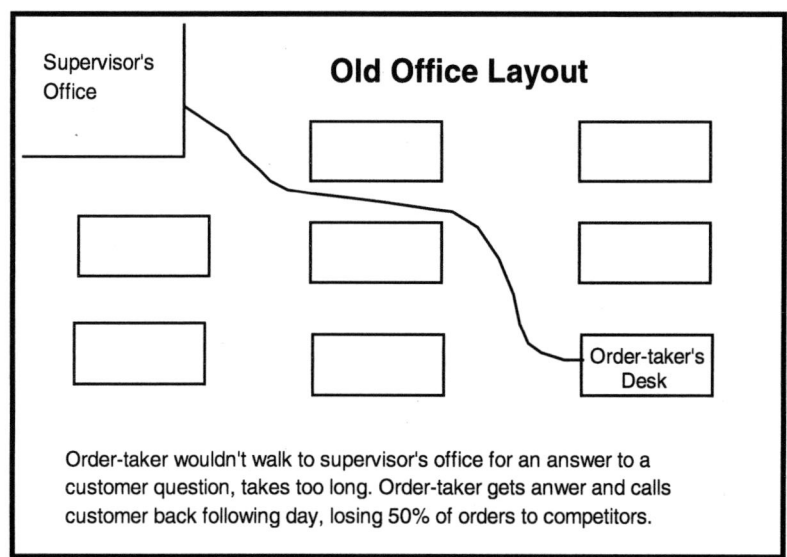

Next, the company decided to find out what happened to the order rate when the order-taker didn't know the answer to a caller's question and stated they would find out and call them back within 24 hours. Isn't that the standard we all hold ourselves to? The company found out that each time the order taker didn't

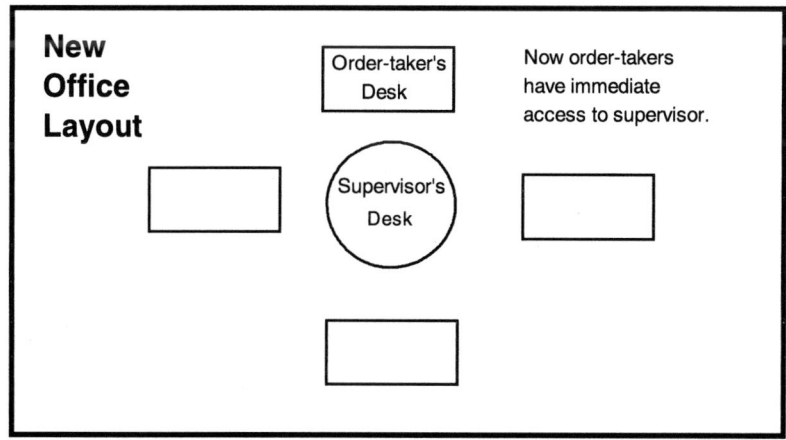

know the answer, and had to find out and call the customer back, the order rate went down by 50 percent. So, after two unanswered questions, the company captured only 25 percent of the orders, even though the order taker was calling the customer back. So, why would the order rate go down? Answer: Because customers get psychic income by crossing that item off their "to-do" list, even though a follow-up study revealed the purchase price from a competitor was usually slightly higher and the quality rarely better.

So the question became, "How do we answer all the customer's questions and capture 100 percent of the orders?" First, was to educate the order-takers on the company's products. This required a radical change in how management thought of the cost of training the order-takers. Instead of an expense, the training cost had to be viewed as an investment (even though training costs are still expensed, of course). Second, the layout of the order taking department had to be reconfigured.

Prior to the study, the departments were arranged in typical fashion. The supervisor's office was in the power position, in the corner (see Old Office Layout diagram, page 15). But this prevented the order-takers from getting the information they needed to answer the customer's question. So, the company rearranged the department, putting the supervisor, the person with the most knowledge, in the middle, with the order-takers arranged like wagon wheel spokes around the supervisor (see New Office Layout diagram, page 15). This layout gives the order-taker immediate access to critical information. Rarely does the company now lose an order because no one knows the answer.

Think about it. You have the item in stock, and your personnel can perform the service. So why would you risk losing a sale because someone doesn't know the answer to a customer question. In fact, you can't afford NOT to train your receptionist or order-takers.

> **Accountants would much rather be exactly wrong, than approximately right.**

If yours is an accounting firm, does the receptionist know, in detail, what every member of the firm does, so calls can be routed to the right person the first time? Are you losing revenue because potential customers are hanging up in frustration?

Again, the cost of such training is easy to measure, yet the benefit of the training is much more difficult to measure. As a profession, accountants will measure something to the nth

degree, even if it's not as relevant as something that is much more difficult to quantify — like customer satisfaction.

Think back to the last education class you attended. At the time you registered for the class, you knew exactly what the cost was (you wrote or signed the check), and decided that the benefit exceeded the cost, even though you could not quantify the benefit. World-class companies apply this same philosophy to all their operations.

Phone Statistics:

Executives spend 15 minutes a day or 60 hours a year on hold. — *USA Today*, August 1990.

34% of callers who hang up will not call back. *Voice Response, Inc.*

88% of callers preferred on-hold messages to other hold options, and 16-20% made a purchase based on an on-hold offer. Stan Rapp and Tom Collins of MAXIMARKETING, an independent research firm.

. . . 85% of callers put on hold keep listening if there's a message. *INBOUND/OUTBOUND*, April 1989.

Lan Chile Airline says its call-abandon rate decreased 50% when the company began running promotional messages to callers on hold. *INBOUND/OUTBOUND*, February 1989.

Nationwide Insurance found that when it played promotional messages, the time callers stayed on the line increased 130%. *INBOUND/OUTBOUND*, February 1989.

94% of all marketing budgets are spent to induce a customer to call, and only 6% to handle the call once it is received. The Inbound Telephone Call Center, Fall 1990.

The problem is linkage

This brings us to the difficult part; linking changes in non-financial performance measures to the bottom line. For example, if you improve customer satisfaction by five percent, what will happen to profits? Unfortunately, we don't have the tools to answer that question with any degree of accuracy, if at all.

However, interesting work is being done in this area. For example, in 1988 Xerox did a base line survey of 10,000 of its customers to find out how they rated it on a scale of "1" to "5". Customers that gave Xerox a "1" were extremely dissatisfied. These customers were labeled "terrorist", because

> **As a profession, accountants will measure something to the nth degree, even if it's not as relevant as something that is much more difficult to quantify — like customer satisfaction.**

unhappy customers tell many people how terrible the company is. At the other end of the scale, customers who rated Xerox a "5" were called "apostles." Customers so happy they are a built-in sales force. Xerox's plan was to raise every customer's satisfaction one level. That is, raise the 1's to 2's, 2's to 3's, and so forth.

Xerox began to survey 10,000 customers each month to track changes in satisfaction. In 1991, the process was stopped to see if there was any correlation between satisfaction and how likely a customer was to do business with Xerox again. Everyone had always assumed it was a linear relationship. That is, a customer who rated Xerox a "2" was twice as likely to be a repeat customer as one which rated Xerox a "1". Thus, it was thought that a customer giving Xerox a "5" rating would be five times more likely to buy again.

However, as shown by the exponential revenue line in the Customer Satisfaction Drives Loyalty Drives Profits graph on page 21, Xerox found that the relationship was not linear at all. In fact, a customer giving a "5" rating was **six** times more likely to do more business with Xerox than a customer giving a "4" rating. Knowing this, how would you deploy your limited resources for customer satisfaction? When I ask this question in class, most people say, "Spend the money on level '4'

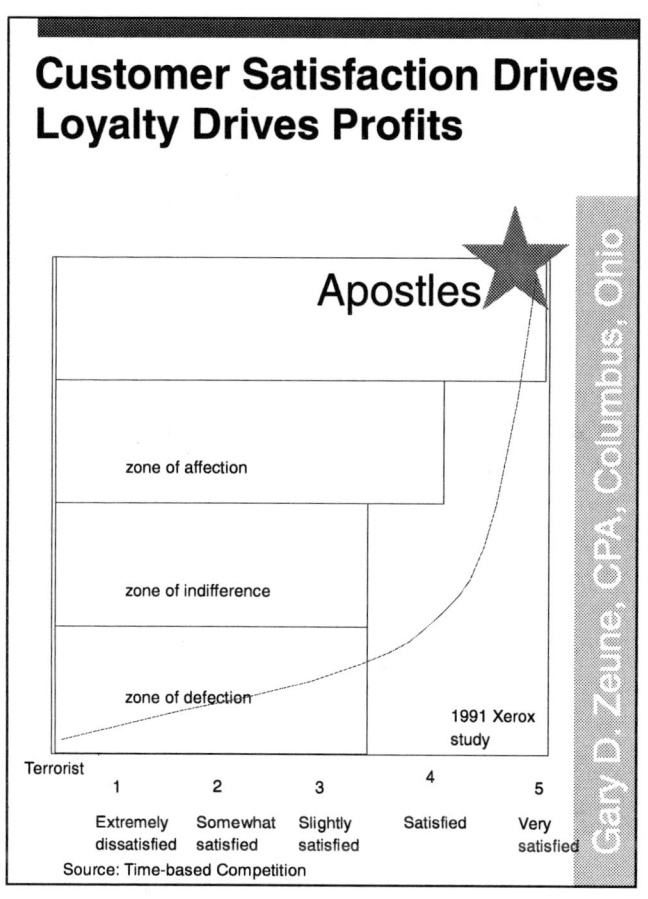

customers," to move them to "5" level customers. Wrong! First, "5" level, very satisfied customers, must be retained. They are so profitable you must make certain they stay satisfied. Customers which give you a "5" must be taken care of. Next, devote your remaining resources to moving the "4" level customers to the "5" level. But why work so hard to move a "4" level customer to a "5" level? Because "4" level customers stay with you only because they don't have a good reason to leave. A reason to leave can be either you doing something wrong, or competitors enticing your customer away.

But what do you do with the 1's, 2's and 3's? Fire them. That's right, fire your customers! Why? If yours is the average American company, the best 20 percent of your customers account for 80 percent of your profits. The middle 60 percent of your customers add another 30 to 40 percent of profits. But how can you have over 100 percent profits? Because you lose your shirt on the bottom 20 percent of your customers. Why? Because your worst customers are extremely price sensitive, willing to wait extraordinary long lead times for your product or service, and demand a significantly disproportionate amount of support services.

But, how do you fire your customers? Raise prices. What are the two things that can happen if you raise prices? One, the customers can pay them, and become profitable. Or, they can leave. Either way, your company is better off. Think about it this way. One of your most powerful competitive weapons is to give your competitors all of your worst customers!

I was in the middle of explaining the concept at one of my classes, and out of the blue one of the participants said, "My God, that's what they're doing." Of course, the class stopped in mid-sentence, wanting to know what the secret was.

"Jim," the CPA attending my course, was the CFO of a liquid petroleum gas distributor. His company was the second largest LP distributor in its market. Jim related that for the prior year or so, his company had been getting many small accounts from its largest competitor. He had been to a half-dozen courses trying to figure out why the competitor was acting this way. He was very worried, because his company had never had so many customers, and was at the same time making less money than it ever had. He then realized that the competitor was trying to run him out of business by giving up all the small accounts. His competitor had computed *Return on Customer* and knew the customer profile required for a customer to be profitable.

Rewarding the Sales Force

This raises the issue of how we reward our sales force. Many companies have a two-tier incentive pay structure. Higher for new customers, lower for existing customers. Based on the above discussions of the profitability of very satisfied existing customers, isn't the traditional sales force pay system dysfunctional? Wouldn't it make much more sense to reverse the com-

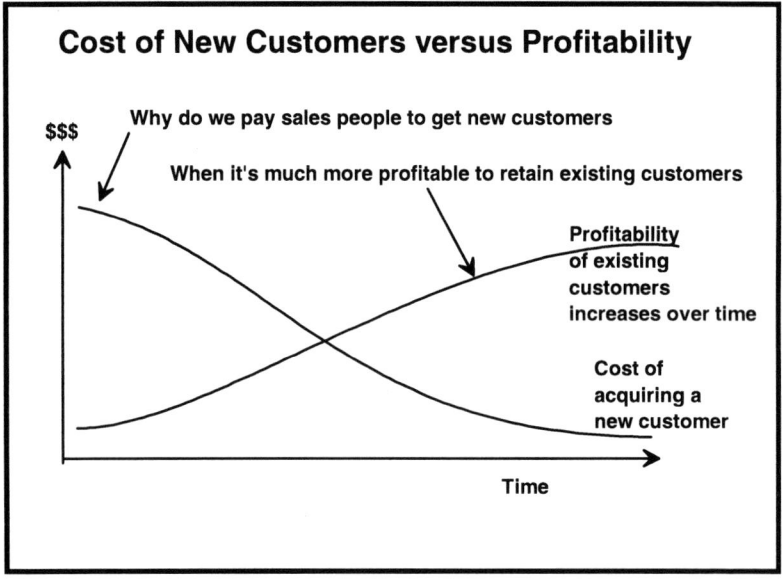

pensation system to reward the sales force to take care of your most profitable — usually long-term — customers?

The sales compensation system at most companies is completely backwards. We pay sales people *more* to get new customers than to keep old ones happy. Consider the implications of the Cost of New Customers vs. Profitability diagram. It is well known that it is 4 to 6 times more expensive to get a new customer than to keep an existing customer. The graph depicts the fact, that on average, the vast majority of effort is in getting a new customer. Even though there is significant front end investment to capture a new customer, and the customer may not become profitable for a long period of time, we reward our sales force to bring in new customers. We should be rewarding our sales forces to keep existing customers, the "5s" in the Xerox study, happy.

> **Accountants must expand from telling management how many "beans" there are, and start telling management where the "beans" *come from*.**

When we reward our sales forces more to get new customers, we reward them for their effort. We should be rewarding them for the result we want — keeping existing, high profit, customers happy. Our sales compensation system is backwards because we don't know the profile of our most profitable customers.

Develop that profile for your customers. BancOne, Columbus, Ohio, recently found that ". . . 20% of its customers provided all of the bank's profits, while 80% of its customers actually cost the bank money."[2] The ultimate source of your profitability is not your products and services, it's your customers. Find out who your current customers are. What is their

---

[2] "Know Thy Customer," *The Wall Street Journal*, Manager's Journal, Duncan McDougall, August 7, 1995.

purchasing pattern? How long have they been a customer? Does their order volume reflect any trend? What's their growth rate? And, what's the profitability, or gross margin, of each customer below the line? To compute customer profitability, you will need to trace every below-the-line dollar to the customer that consumes it. That means instituting some form of activity-based costing.

Mission Statements

Write your company's mission statement here: _____
_____
_____
_____
_____
_____

If what you wrote down has anything to do with your company's product or service -- that is wrong. Why? Because thinking of your business in the context of products or services is an internal focus. By human nature, you focus on effort. Customers don't care about effort, they only care about results. Also, if your mission statement said anything about making money, I want you to think of profits as the *result* of being in business, not the *reason* for being in business.

A typical mission statement is, *"This company provides the highest quality products and services that surpass our customers requirements, on time and at lowest cost."* Here's the BIG picture question: How do you know you are meeting your mission statement? What do you measure, how often, in what level of detail, and in what type of reports? Most companies have mission statements. Very few know whether they are meeting them. Write down three things you measure, outside the financial statements, that tell you whether you are meeting your mission statement:

1)_____
2)_____
3)_____

Goal Congruence

What prevents companies from accomplishing their mission statements? We make the mistake of asking for behavior "A," then rewarding behavior "B." By doing so, we create goal discongruance. We put an employee in the position of conflict when making decisions. For example, say you have a fast-track manager who has just taken over an old plant. The manager has been rising quickly through the ranks, known for fast decisions. The plant has been operating with old, worn out, equipment. Requiring significant maintenance, the plant supervisor approaches the new manager and proposes to spend $5 million to buy all new equipment for the plant.

Accountants provide a lot of data, but very little *information* that front-line employees can *act on*.

At this company, capital budgeting proposals come from the bottom up. The company's hurdle rate is 17 percent, and the supervisors computations show the equipment proposal has a 22 percent return on investment (ROI). After several weeks the supervisor approaches the plant manager asking whether management is willing to buy the new equipment. The manager responds, "I don't know, I didn't send the proposal to headquarters." The supervisor walks away scratching his head, discouraged, unable to figure out why he had failed in his attempt to make a good impression on the new plant manager.

Why wouldn't the manager forward the proposal to headquarters for approval? What the supervisor didn't know was that the manager's compensation included a significant bonus element, based on plant profitability. Nor was the supervisor aware that the manager was anticipating being there only a couple of years. Because the plant used accelerated depreciation, the manager's pay would decline during his short tenure. The pay system put the manager in a conflict position regarding the equipment decision. If the manager did what was good for the company, his pay would suffer. If the manager took care of himself, the company would suffer (the company's ROI will be less than it otherwise would be if the equipment is purchased).

The goal discongruance is caused by the ROI analysis being long-term (usually 10+ years) versus the manager's personal analysis being short-term (probably two or three years).

Another common example can be found in purchasing departments. Many companies pay their purchasing agents a base salary and a percentage of any savings for purchases below some standard amount.

Would accountants do their jobs differently if they had to come to the office every day and "sell" their reports to the rest of the organization?

The consequence is that purchasing agents will attempt to buy "cheap", even if the company has quality standards. A major appliance manufacturer found that every time a defect went undetected one more step in the chain, the cost of fixing it increased 10-fold. For example, if a load of defective nuts and bolts is discovered on the loading dock, the cost of returning them and getting new ones was 3 cents a set. If the defective nuts and bolts go into inventory, the cost of replacing them is 30 cents. If they get onto the manufacturing floor, the cost is $3. If not detected on the manufacturing floor, and the defect is detected at the end of the production line, the cost is $30. If the defect isn't detected in the factory, and the appliance is repaired in the customer's home, the cost is $300. Can you afford to have frequent defects in your products or services? No.

To achieve maximum returns, companies must make certain that every measurement system and reward system is *goal congruent*. In other words, when a manager makes a decision, the decision should be beneficial for both the company and the manager, or detrimental for both. Otherwise the company will operate at a suboptimum level.

Product Development

When we develop new products, the accounting focus is usually on whether or not the company is within the development budget. This is an accurate, but very shortsighted view. In one study, the effects on the life-time profitability of other factors was analyzed. As illustrated in the graph Factors Affecting Profits on page 31, in an industry represented by 20 percent annual growth, 12 percent annual price increases in a five-year product

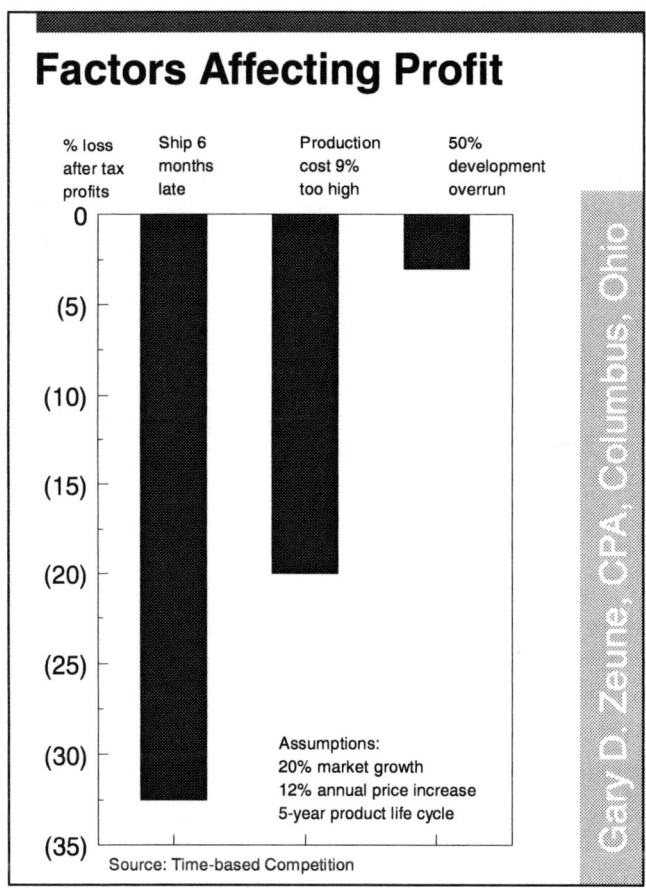

life-cycle, a 50 percent overrun in development costs decreased life-time profits by less than five percent. If, to stay within the development budget, the company develops a poor product design and production costs are nine percent too high, life-time profits decline by about 20 percent. But, in a fast paced industry that was the subject of the study, getting a new product to market six months late resulted in a profit loss of between 30 and 35 percent. Again, what's not in the financial statements is more important than what is.

Focusing on development costs results in a precise measure, but it's not nearly as significant as the lost profits. If production costs are too high, we short-cut the development to come in under budget, or came to market behind competitors. Accountants are good at measuring what is right in front of them, but not very good at measuring what isn't there. This is an example of how accountants would much rather be exactly wrong, than approximately right.

A personal example. Several years ago, I had a consulting client that distributed marine paint to boat repair shops. The luxury tax had been enacted. The boating industry was suffering, my client included. "How do you compete?" I asked. "Price. Everybody is always beating me up on price," he responded. I then asked how he knew this was the right basis of competition. He got a funny look on his face and responded he had been in the business for over 25 years and knew that price was most important because that's what his customers always asked about.

Next, I asked where his sales came from. "I sell paint," he said again, with a funny look on his face (he's thinking I'm an idiot at this point). I said, "No, I mean, how much of each color and brand of paint do you sell." He said he sold about 150 varieties of paint, but had no idea which varieties resulted in what sales. An analysis showed the 80/20 rule applied. That is, 30 varieties of paint (20% of the 150 varieties) accounted for 80 percent of sales.

I then decided to talk to a few long-time customers and ask one question, "What's important to you in doing business with my client?" In the top ten reasons, where do you think price was? That's right, near the bottom. The number one attribute customers deemed most important was *speed of delivery*. My client didn't understand that when his customer had to repair a boat, if the shop didn't have the right paint in stock, it cost the repair shop over $300 to back the boat out and bring another one in to repair. Speed of delivery could solve his customers' problem.

Knowing that speed of delivery is most important, and that 20 percent of the paint varieties represented 80 percent of sales, what would your competitive strategy be? The one we came up with was to become the Domino's of marine paint distribution. My client bought several additional vans, equipped each with a cellular phone, two gallons of each of the 30 varieties of paint, sent flyers to all the repair shops in town promising 30 minute delivery, and raised prices! When the alternative costs $300, a few extra dollars a gallon is insignificant to the repair shop.

Another example. I had a small trucking company as a client. The company was a mini-UPS, but handled mostly fragile items, such as glass and crystal. The employees were very careful, rarely breaking anything, but because they were on salary, they also were not very productive. To boost productivity, the owner put the employees on a piece work pay system. Productivity soared, but what else soared? Breakage. And the number of packages shipped to wrong addresses sky-rocketed. The owner, very frustrated by this point, was about to institute a punishment system where, when something was broken, he would figure out who had done the deed, and take it out of the responsible employee's pay. I asked him, "How do you think the employees are going to react when you walk into the warehouse and ask who dropped a box off the shelf and broke the crystal vase inside?" He thought for a moment and admitted that employees would blame each other. So a negative punishment system would not work without employee morale suffering and business declining.

What about rewarding employees individually? Again, it won't work. Employees will compete with each other for the bonus, rather than taking care of the customer. What to do then? How about rewarding all the employees when an entire week goes by without an error? Now what kind of behavior do you drive? Team-work. Why? Because either everyone gets a bonus, or no one gets a bonus. And, the owner found he didn't have to spend nearly as much time in the warehouse because the employees would figure out how to serve the customer. Employees would not tolerate a lazy or careless fellow employee. It cut into their bonuses.

Why Do You Carry Inventory?

The textbook answers usually include, among others: just in case a customer places an order, in case the first item picked is defective, to absorb overhead, to keep the plants running at an even capacity.

What if I said that you carry inventory to compensate for your inefficiencies?

Think of the amount of inventory you carry as the water level in a lake. Your customer is in a boat on one side of the lake and needs to get to the other side. If you start lowering the water level, your inventory, the customer's boat will crash on

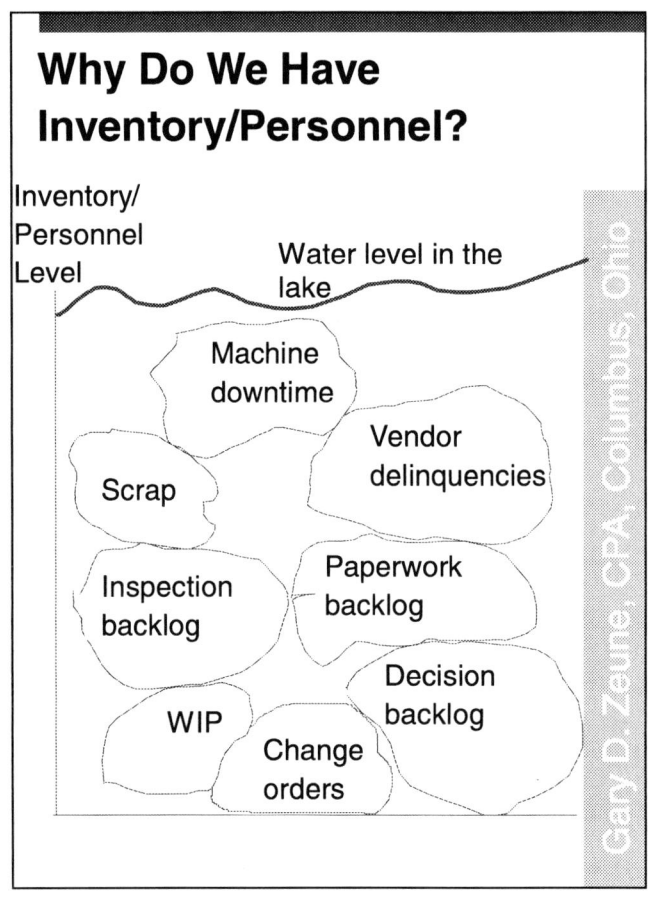

the rocks of inefficiency. As depicted in the Why We Have Inventory/Personnel graph above, most inefficiencies are obvious: machine downtime, vendor delinquencies, scrap, inspection and paperwork backlog, work-in-process and change orders because of faulty specifications. The most important inefficiency is the most easily measured -- decision backlog. Have you ever measured how long it takes to get a decision made in your company? Create a form to track decision-making time and give one to every employee. Just by tracking how long it takes to make decisions, you will make them faster. This is a very powerful competitive weapon.

Does Reengineering Work?

In the fall of 1994, the Institute of Management Accountants surveyed over 3000 members about their reengineering efforts. The survey covered primarily small and midsize companies to determine the current state-of-the art.

By and large, reengineering efforts are being championed by the CEO and CFO (see Who's the Champion). This is as it should be. If the CEO assigned anyone else, it would signal the employees that the

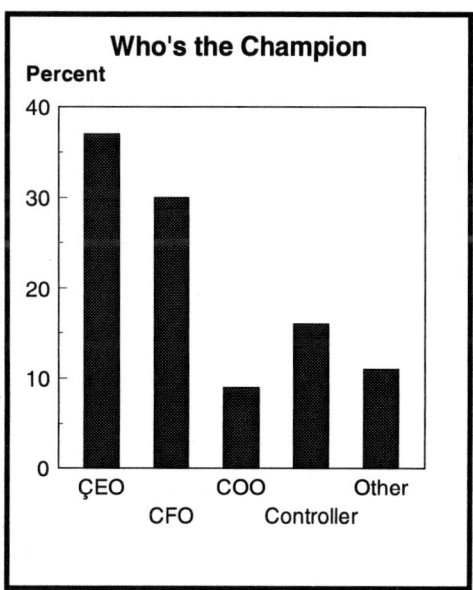

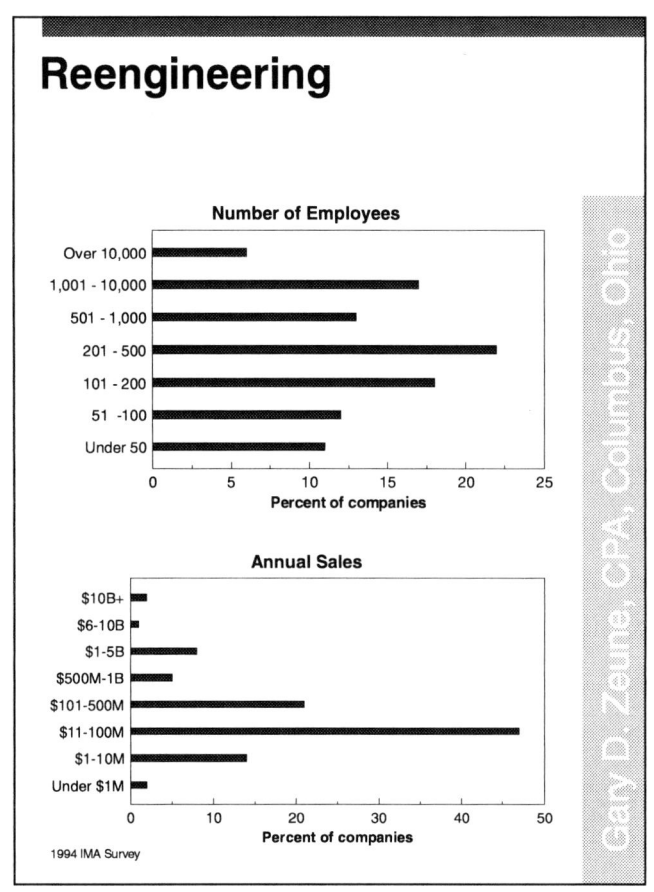

effort isn't important enough to warrant the CEO's attention. As a result, most employees won't pay much attention to it. Then, when it doesn't work, the employees become even more resistant to the next "management technique" of the month. Their attitude becomes, "Ignore it, it'll go away in a couple of months."

Nearly 60 percent of the companies reported that reengineering has made a significant contribution to the company. But, since nearly 40 percent of the companies had started their reengineering efforts in the two years prior to the survey, about 25 percent reported it was too early to tell whether the effort would produce results. As the Reengineering graph on page 38 shows, the survey primarily involved small and mid-size companies.

> **Customers don't care when you ship their order. Customers only care when they receive it. Are you measuring the wrong thing?**

Many people think of reengineering as downsizing, but the IMA survey showed that simply isn't true. The vast majority of companies re-engineered to better serve customers, increase productivity, or improve business processes. And about half of The companies reported using an outside consultant to assist the effort.

The graph on page 40, Reengineering: Tools Used, shows the techniques used by companies to redesign their processes. Reengineering uses a variety of tools: benchmarking,

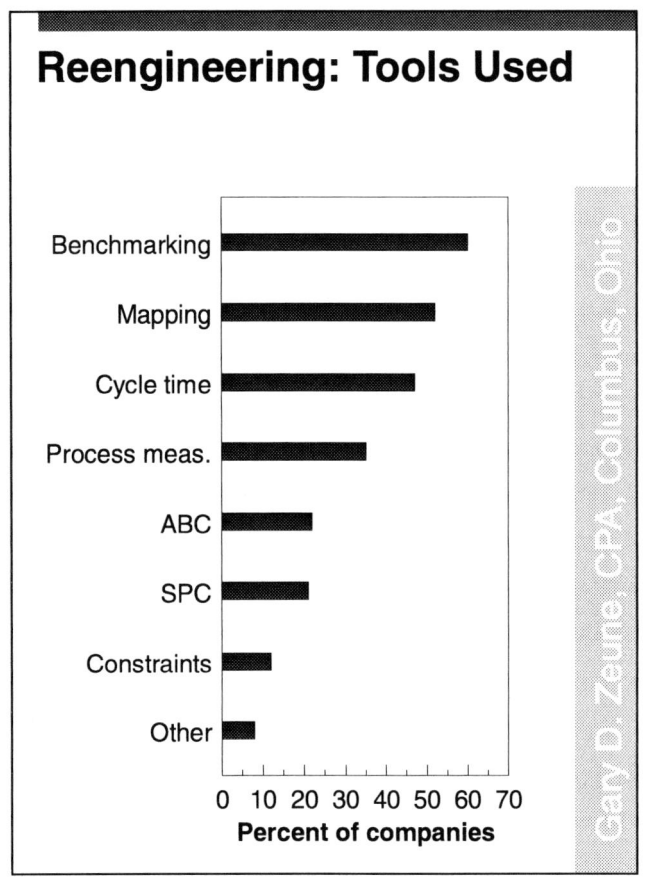

mapping, cycle time, process measurement, activity based costing, statistical process control, and theory of constraints.

Successful Reengineering

Factor	Percent helped by factor
Good communications	100
Strong mandate	95
Intermediate goals and deadlines	95
Adaptive plan	91
Adequate resources	86
Urgency of change	86
Performance measures	84
Early, tangible results	76
Customers and suppliers	62
Benchmarking	62

Reengineering for Profit, Price Waterhouse, 1994

What it takes to reengineer

Good communication is the key to successful reengineering. Who says so? Price Waterhouse. PW's 1994 survey of the

CEOs of companies which have successfully re-engineered, found that only one reengineering technique shows up on the radar screen — last in the list — benchmarking. Yet, most people spend their time trying to figure out which technique to use. Most techniques will work if properly used.

Successful Reengineering lists the top reasons companies succeed at reengineering their operations.

It's time to reengineer finance and accounting

Have you ever thought of your finance function as a provider of services to its internal customers? If not, you better. Have you rethought every step of every operation? In "The New Blueprint for Finance," *CFO Magazine* profiled several companies that have re-engineered their finance function and reaped tremendous returns in the process. In the next 10 years, continuous reengineering will become a competitive necessity. To reengineer your finance or accounting function, you must adopt Peter Drucker's philosophy, "There is nothing less useful than to do a little better that which should not be done at all." CFOs are rethinking the way finance should operate. The goal is to help senior management set strategy, not simply reduce the time spent on mindless tasks.

One company that has re-engineered for competitive superiority is Pfizer Inc. CFO David Shedlarz asked one question, "How can finance help to provide a competitive advantage?" An advocate of reform, he added, "Change is opportunity, not a threat."

For example, Shedlarz has a 12-foot map of the 5,000 hours spent on Pfizer's federal tax return. When mapped, it was obvious non-value-added activities wasted about 25% of the 5,000 hours! Time is wasted by waiting for data, checking, and double checking information. Get rid of these activities so your accountants can spend this time on more interesting and strategic tax planning areas.

John Owens, CFO of Phillips Fibers Corp., a $180 million company in Greenberg, South Carolina, wanted to get a handle on the key concepts of reengineering :

- "Eliminate wasteful, irrelevant, redundant steps in such transaction-based activities as invoice processing.
- "Use such technologies as data warehouses and client/server networks to consolidate accounting centers and reduce costs and staff.
- "Change the flow of work so people can spend time on value-added analysis.

- "Provide business managers with meaningful measures of operational efficiency."

Greg Hackett, President of The Hackett Group in Cleveland, says we must reevaluate elements we've always required in our system of checks and balances. For example, you have a salesman who is bringing in several million dollars of business each year, and you won't cut him an expense check until a clerk makes certain he didn't charge a $10 video to the room. Is checking the sales person's expense report for minor items time well spent, or could it be used in a higher value activity?

You must be willing to examine every step of every process and ask: "Do I get any value from the effort?" Most companies don't undertake reengineering until there's a substantial drop in business or competition begins taking market share. However, if in real trouble, you don't have time to test how well your finance department operates. The acid test to see if your reports are important: Try to sell the information or reports to the departments that you currently provide them to. If they are not willing to pay, why are you creating them?

Last summer, I walked uptown to the flower shop three blocks from my home in Worthington, Ohio to buy my daughter a birthday card. I picked out a card, walked to the cash register, but there wasn't anyone there. I heard voices in the back and stuck my head around the corner. Several people were working on flower arrangements, looked up, smiled, and went back to work. I laid the card down on the counter (to let the cashier know someone had been there), and started to leave. Suddenly a man, who had been looking at some ceramic items on the other side of the store, asked if he could help me. I assumed he was a customer. The owner, he walked behind the register counter, wrote down "1 birthday card - $1.75" on a pad, punched $1.75 into the register, pushed the "Card" button, took my $2, and gave me change.

I turned to leave, but couldn't resist. I asked why he wrote the information on the pad. He said because his accountant told him it was needed to make certain no one was stealing. I asked him if his employees weren't smart enough to figure out all they had to do to steal was write "$1.50" on the pad, ring up "$1.50" on the register, and put 25 cents in their pocket. He admitted they probably had long ago figured that out, but still, accounting said they need the information was required.

Then, I asked if he had ever noticed how many customers, frustrated with the long lines and slow check-out time, would simply put their purchases down and walk out. He said he had noticed, but thought they were loyal customers who would shop in nearby stores, and return later. I told him they probably would shop nearby, at the drug or grocery store, which also have nice cards.

Finally, I asked, "What do you know as a result of writing the information on the pad that you didn't know already from the information that was keyed into the register?" He answered, "I must be doing something right, because I'm the 43rd largest independent flower shop in the country." I replied, "There must be a reason you're only the 43rd largest flower shop in the country."

In 1987, DuPont conducted one of the first benchmarking studies of finance. But it wasn't until a 21% decline in second quarter earnings that the effort became serious, forced by a $1 billion reduction in staff. Because of the benchmarking study, DuPont expects to cut finance costs by 40 to 45% by the end of the year.

Robert Gunn, president of Gunn Howell Morkos Partners, and one time partner of Hackett, warns CFOs to "avoid sinking money into new technology before planning how to streamline, simplify, and standardize. The mistake in the past has been to automate the useless work, when the answer, in fact, is to eliminate it."

Champion International Senior management told CFO Jack Nimons that the controllers needed to ". . . do better analysis and be better business partners." Champion needed to streamline the tracking of costs and adopt non-financial performance measures that would help managers grow their units. To help, the company called John Shank, a professor of managerial accounting [and frequent speaker on activity-based costing at AICPA conferences] at Dartmouth's Amos Tuck Graduate School of Business. Shank immediately recognized Champion's cumbersome cost accounting system with "painfully detailed profit projections" as a major impediment to reengineering.

Shank taught the plant number controllers to produce more meaningful reports. It didn't work. The accountants forgot to "sell" the reports to the plant personnel. Shank began tracking how the reports were used. The accountants said they prepared the highly detailed planned versus actual reports because operations wanted

> **Try to sell the information or reports to the departments that you currently provide them to. If they are not willing to pay, why are you creating them?**

them. The mill workers claimed the mill managers needed them. But, the yard workers tracked key information on scraps of paper (i.e., the accounting reports were useless). The mill managers said their unit bosses needed the information, who in turn said the mill managers were the ones needing the information. Shank concluded, "Everyone said someone else uses it, but the truth is, *nobody did* [emphasis added]. You had managers working 60 to 70 hours a week producing reports that didn't help people."

Convinced he would have to throw out the old before adapting the new, Ninoms installed a new controller and mill manager in Champion's oldest plant in Hamilton, Ohio. The plant produced 1,500 premium product lines, such as magazine stock. For a slimmed down, more responsive system, the controller held "head-banging sessions" with operations to develop meaningful performance measures. Twelve critical success measures were developed: "lead time, scrap rates, first-pass yields, work-in-process inventories, customer satisfaction . . ." One piece of paper replaced reams of paper each month.

> "The mistake in the past has been to automate the useless work, when the answer, in fact, is to eliminate it."
> **Robert Gunn, President**
> **Gunn Howell Morkos Partners**

With the nonfinancial performance measures in place, the plant was able to make the switch to shorter production runs to stay in sync with customer demands. The result? Increased profits of 33% the first year.

> ... most companies could double their profits by retaining just 5% of the customers they lose!

Johnson & Johnson (J&J) joined DuPont in the pioneering benchmarking study in 1987. CFO Clark Johnson learned that his finance department budget was 2.7% of revenues, versus the group's average of 2.1%. "The first thing we did was deny it — Oh, well, we're different." By consolidating payroll and accounts payable, adopting a single general ledger system and chart of accounts, finance costs are now 1.9% of revenues, while volume is up 30%. He hopes to get to 1% by decade end. Johnson said, "Without benchmarking, we would have never thought that was possible."

For "top-of-the-mind" awareness, J&J finance staff's PCs greet them each morning with, "Influence the right business decisions . . . to exceed competitors' growth in shareholder value and cash flow . . ." For example, J&J benchmarked its payables area. J&J could process 7,700 invoices annually per employee versus 30,000 at Federal Express and Wal-Mart. J&J

started capturing information by vendor, automatically matching POs with invoices, widening tolerances to several hundred dollars, and auditing on a statistical basis.

The annual budget for staff functions at J&J corporate headquarters is another area of effort. In 1992, it took 174 days. J&J is shooting for 30, by eliminating handwritten worksheets, streamlining data entry, dropping detailed allocations of overhead for floor space, and rounding dollar amounts to the nearest thousand.

TRW, Inc. CFO Peter Hellman agrees with the reengineering gurus who advise, "Pick the low-hanging fruit." When starting your reengineering effort, usually through benchmarking, go after the easy targets and score early wins to build momentum. If you do, people will embrace, rather than just accept, the changes. Employees become more important to the company. Hellman also notes it takes patience for the process to work.

Having joined TRW as treasurer in 1989 and becoming CFO in 1991, Hellman asked an important question: "If design time for satellites is down from five years to three, and automotive scrap rates have been reduced materially, shouldn't finance also look at improving quality and customer satisfaction?"

TRW started downsizing in 1986, with the headcount going from 30,000 to 20,000. With fewer people in finance to do more work, Hellman boosted productivity by eliminating meaningless tasks, speeding up work practices and getting people to think creatively about their work. After spending the first year on introspection, a TQM coordinator was brought in to identify major processes and bring a customer-service mentality to the finance people in their dealings with operations. They also learned cycle time. The improvement teams learned not to point fingers when they uncovered unnecessary work and reports. Instead, they learned to eliminate it.

Hellman overhauled internal audit last year. Previously, once the auditors left the field, it took an average of 88 days to produce a final report that included management's responses and an action plan. Of course, the information was "old news" to operations by that time. In addition, audits were disruptive, with their insatiable appetite for data and adversarial exit conference. Internal audit was viewed as the "finance police."

As a result of the overhaul, internal audit is now viewed as a customer service. Armed with laptop PCs, reports get out in an average of 10 days. If a problem is spotted, the auditor must write up a preliminary memo so the line manager can respond immediately. In addition, auditors must now send letters listing the documents to be reviewed 30 to 60 days in advance.

Ron Vargo, TRW VP and Treasurer, surveyed his "customers" and found they didn't know much about his function. He made a list of treasury services to every department available. As a result, "people in operations said they wanted to see more of us, not less."

Noting that the cost of transaction processing varies from $3.80 to $9.80, Hellman's next step is to provide each operation with reports highlighting the differences. "I won't have to push shared services; it will happen. I have to let the market decide. I wish this whole process wouldn't have to take five years, but in the end, it works better to let the guy out in the unit see that someone else is doing better. The data becomes compelling."

You might want to consider subscribing to this publication. It's excellent and complementary. Write CFO Magazine, PO Box 381, Mt. Morris, IL 61504-8071, or call 617-345-9700.

Quality: Perception and Profits

Management and customers have vastly different views on quality efforts. The Quality Research Institute reported the following results of a survey conducted for it by quality guru Philip Crosby (Associates) and the Gallup Organization. The Institute randomly surveyed 3,000 customers of the retail and hospitality industries. In addition, customers and executives of public utilities were interviewed where customers had no choice in the service provider.

The results were the same regardless of the industry. The key sentence for understanding the survey is: *Management focused on its efforts; customers focused on results. It's all too easy to forget customers are unaware and generally do not care how much effort management puts into satisfying their needs.*

Customers are looking for satisfaction. The company that satisfies its customers' needs will get their business. Try this on for size: 86% of the 3,000 customers surveyed think business leaders do not pay much attention to quality, but are more concerned with profits. Is it possible this is the result of not being satisfied?

Ninety-three percent of department store managers and 78% of discount store managers said their firms were committed to quality service. Consumers gave retail companies a mid-50% score. A vast difference in perception. Of the 1,402 customers of the hotel/motel industry who were surveyed, approximately 40% rated the industry as meeting their needs most of the time. Contrast that with the 70% of the 102 hotel/motel executives who said they were meeting customer needs.

Throughout the survey, customers consistently said they would shop at a store or stay at a hotel if better service was provided. In contrast, a majority of the executives indicated cost and merchandise are the two most important factors in attracting customers. Are managers talking to their customers? This suggests customers expect cost and merchandise selection as givens, and that service is what differentiates them.

Customers of utilities, cable, natural gas, local telephone and electric companies don't think highly of their companies' services either. Of the lot, the highest score, but still only 37% of the 1,001 customers surveyed, went to electric utilities. And only 19% of these customers think their electric company showed a genuine interest in them. It's a good thing utilities have a monopoly!

What's the problem here? It's our focus. We tend to put our spotlight on our efforts, not the results we are getting out of our efforts! You will be sadly disappointed with the dollars spent if you measure the wrong thing to gauge your success. You need to measure results, not effort. Measure your efforts to see if it was worth the investment. For example, success isn't measured by how many employees you send through TQM training. That is easy to measure. Success is measured by the positive impact it is having. The financial impact of much success, such as improving satisfaction, is difficult, but critical, to measure.

As recently reported in a *Harvard Business Review* study, "...customer defections have a surprisingly powerful impact on the bottom line. [Defections] can have more to do with a service company's profits than scales [of economies], market share, unit costs, and many other factors usually associated with a competitive advantage." The issue is "lifetime value." Consider the following reasons customers defect to a new vendor:

Reasons Customers Defect[3]

Customer moves	9%
Go to competitor	9
Poorly handled complaints	14
No special reason	68
Total	100%

---

[3] *U.S. News and World Report*

This study shows, with a little work, we could probably retain 91% of the lost customers. Even those with "No special reason." These customers weren't satisfied. It wasn't that these customers had a reason to leave, they simply didn't have a reason to stay. You must give customers a *compelling* reason to stay. Satisfying their needs isn't enough. You must exceed customer expectations. Have you ever computed the cost of obtaining a new customer? It's almost always cheaper to retain a customer! The HBR study noted that most companies could double their profits by retaining just 5% of the customers they lose!

How can that be? Most customers require you to make your money the old fashion way. You must earn it. At first, a customer will do a little business with you. Then, as their confidence in you grows, their orders grow in value. Concurrently, as you become more familiar with the account, the cost of servicing that customer declines as a percentage of the value of the order. You become more efficient at servicing a long-time customer which makes perfect sense. And, if you're really good, new customers will arrive from word of mouth advertising. To operate in this high pressure environment, here are three simple thoughts:

1. *Communicate.* If you wait until you see dissatisfied customers show up on the bottom line, it's too late. They are gone — probably forever! Customers almost never voluntarily tell you when they are dissatisfied, but I recently read somewhere they tell an average of 14 other people. How do you know if they are satisfied? Ask, by mailing short questionnaires; setting up a toll-free number for questions; making certain your address and phone number is on every piece of paper you give them (including your ads). Also, this allows you to build a data-base for direct-mail marketing.
2. *Make it personal.* Start a newsletter to announce sales, store policies, personnel changes, anything that might interest your customers (and don't guess - ask what interests them). Include coupons and answer customer letters. Don't use only the positive ones. Every company gets negative letters. The key is to show how you went out-of-your-way to satisfy the customer. That is more believable than a company that never makes a mistake.
3. *Do more than what's expected -- people will pay for it.* I recently bought a new computer. The company custom builds PCs, and it's prices are 5 to 10% higher than other stores off-the-shelf models. Know why I am willing to pay more? Because, any time I want to make a change, add a CD-ROM drive or new hard drive, the company will install it

free! How can they do this? They know if I buy a new component and try to install it myself, I'll probably screw it up or break something in the process. I'll really be angry if I have to pay them to fix it. They would rather have a happy customer by having their techs spend 10 minutes doing the installation right. Now from whom do you think I'm going to buy my next PC?

Our background and training as financial managers leads us to analyze what we can measure most accurately, whether its the most relevant information or even the best decision — if management could only figure out the value of repeat customer business. My PC vendor hasn't, but I'll guarantee you the owner intuitively knows repeat business is more profitable than charging to install a new component. And, how many people are going to buy a new component somewhere else and take it in for installation? Not many. Net result? The company ends up making many sales it otherwise wouldn't.

A second example is even more dramatic. There's a little company in Eden Prairie, Minnesota, that repairs PC motherboards, mostly IBM. They fix not only what is wrong, but also any other parts that are likely to fail. Then, the company warrants the entire board, not just the repair for an entire year.

How loyal do you think its customers are? Of course, the company has a compensation system that rewards the techs to repair the boards consistent with company policy.

Teams, Not Companies, Win Quality Cups

The Rochester Institute of Technology joined forces with *USA Today* to recognize small teams or individuals for quality in five categories: manufacturing firms, service firms, small organizations, government, and not-for-profit groups. We'll focus on the two winners that made the most significant advances, with the least cost and effort.

Manufacturing   Wood costs were soaring. So, while eating burgers and chocolate cookies on December 19, 1991, ten Boise Cascade employees at the Deridder, Louisiana, plant tried to figure out how they could improve the way newsprint was made.

"In God we trust; all others must have data."

The employees, who usually work days, spent the night in the wood yard counting and sorting the fresh-cut pine and learned some astonishing things. They discovered the plant was using significantly more wood than anyone realized and that usable wood was being diverted into cheap liner board. It took seven months, but the result was an annual savings of at least $1.5 million. The team did something most companies haven't yet learned. First, the team questioned old assumptions, and second, it based decisions on accurate information, not guesswork.

The team members came from three departments; some were managers, others were hourly workers. A consulting firm taught the team to collect and analyze information to pin down the problem. Team member Tommy Linder said, "All these things we'd taken for gospel were absolutely wrong." It always had been assumed the higher the quality of the pine wood, the better the end products: liner board (used in corrugated boxes) and newsprint.

Amazingly, for the first time, tests were conducted on the quality of the wood going into production versus the quality of the newsprint coming out. The team found they could make high-quality paper out of poor-quality wood. Now, the plant no longer uses only 100% ground high-quality wood. It's down to 50%, and might go lower — saving at least $1.5 million per year.

What about all the wood that was being purchased and the plant said it wasn't using? The team found the crane didn't pick up 12 cords (2.7 tons) with each bite. It really picked up 17 cords. Would that throw off your cost computations?

Now the plant has a new motto: "In God we trust; all others must have data."

Small Business Scranton, Pennsylvania-based Fitchbrug Coated Products had been doing business nearly the same for 30 years. Overall, it was making money, but the medical products division was in trouble. Customers were returning 4.5% of the company's products, and employees didn't want to redo the work. Because of this, CEO Brian Kelly started a TQM program in 1991. He formed cross-functional teams to solve problems. He concludes that Fitchburg wouldn't be in the medical products business today if he hadn't formed teams to tackle the problems. The $82 million company has 320 employees and medical products contributes 7%.

> "Your organization and processes are perfectly designed to give you the results you are getting."
> **Author Unknown, Toledo Scale, Columbus, Ohio.**

Kelly set up 27 teams consisting of salesmen, the marketing VP, production workers and customer service people. Teams met weekly to identify problems and formulate solutions.

First, the team devised a system to track what customers wanted. Each customer wanted its tape cut in different lengths and widths, and packaged in a different way. As usual, no one on the production floor knew this.

Team members from the shop floor visited customers to find out how their products were being used and what the problems were. For example, Fitchburg spliced its tape on rolls. This caused the tape to break going through one customer's equipment, shutting down the line. The customer charged the cost back to Fitchburg, and it got expensive. Also, forklifts were damaging tape in storage, ripping the bottom off the 1200-foot roles. At $10 a foot, the company assumed it was a cost of business. One team designed a soft felt cradle to fit over the forklift. Damages are no longer a cost of business.

But the biggest change was in employee attitude. The teams fostered a sense of camaraderie. This maximized the value of the training, including training sessions on how to hold meetings. The company spent $5 million on new equipment to improve production quality, because management knew the teams would make certain it worked. Last, Fitchburg got tough with suppliers that didn't get shipments to customers on time, and reduced the number of shippers it used by 50%. You can reach Fitchburg at (717)347-2035.

How World Class Companies Manage Their Suppliers

With vendors providing 50 to 80 percent of the end value of a product's or service's content, is it any surprise that world class companies (including Baldrige Quality winners) view their relationship with suppliers fundamentally different than the rest of us?

The traditional purchasing model focuses on things. Successful companies focus on people which come together to satisfy the needs of the mutual customers, the end user. Think about your own experience, perhaps with a car you've owned. The auto companies actually manufacture only a small percentage of the parts. But, if the starter fails, you don't ask who manufactured the starter and call that supplier.

How do you refocus from the traditional adversarial system where price is all important to a mutual satisfaction brigade? World class companies have a common view to supplier management.

Manage the Suppliers - Not the Supplies Award contracts to a single supplier that becomes your defacto partner. Trust is an essential ingredient. In some cases, you may have to have an alternate supplier until the primary supplier understands that cooperating will be more profitable. A small equity position can expedite the establishment of the necessary trust.

Constantly changing suppliers for pricing advantage is self-defeating. Multiple suppliers introduce variations. Variations cause problems downstream. Select the best supplier for each job. Have your suppliers compete, and let them know the winner gets a long-term commitment. The competition will drive the suppliers to their best performance. Let the contenders know you expect this performance all the time.

Once selected, begin cooperative efforts to reduce cost. AT&T's Supply Line Management Center has learned that selecting the best supplier maximizes the likelihood of a successful partnership. Look beyond today's price to the lifetime cost. A defective supplier part will result in warranty repairs or service calls far exceeding the small amount saved by choosing a less expensive supplier with inferior quality.

Rate each supplier on the following: Baldrige or other awards, quality history, availability, timeliness, prices, understanding your needs, engineering capabilities, design simplicity, financial stability, susceptibility to strikes, production capacity, delivery capabilities, percent of business you represent, service responsiveness, location, ethics, and quality of supporting operations (e.g., billing).

Select suppliers that see you as the primary customer for that product or service — and you alone. You don't want your suppliers doing business with your competitors. There is no net loss of business. It simply gets redistributed. Your former suppliers now supply competitors -- who are at a competitive disadvantage since you took the best supplier for that part or service.

Satisfy Your Mutual Customer Your and your suppliers jointly work together to satisfy their customers while reducing costs. How? By establishing open communications during all phases of a product's or service's life cycle: design, prototyping, production, delivery, support (e.g., ordering and billing). To make progress, you must share proprietary information so the processes can be integrated from your vendor, to you, and to your customers.

Once selected, you must assure your partners enough business that they can afford to work with you on all phases, as discussed above. A mutual dependence will result that gets away from the antagonistic relationship. Mutually dependent relationships reduce risk and fear. Suppliers become willing to invest in quality improvements because they know they have a customer for the product or service. Xerox, Cadillac and Motorola have suppliers that voluntarily reduce prices.

Partnering is a Two-Way Street A relationship where the supplier provides only steady product flow or quality improvements is not a partnership. The supplier is simply responding to your demands. A partnership enables you and your suppliers to develop a common understanding of customers' needs. Thus, you (plural) can respond quicker as a team. Your suppliers should be able to rate you (in a non-threatening way) as a customer.

In the traditional relationship, customers rarely give their suppliers an opportunity to discuss better ways to serve them, and customers further down the channel. Customers saw products/services as interchangeable commodities. Purchased as cheaply as possible, customers controlled quality by defining performance requirements in contracts. The vendor is seen as a collection of goods and capital rather than an association of people who satisfy customers.

Partnering not only involves your external vendors, it involves every person in every department within your company. When you purchase products/services from an external vendor, your employees expect that product/service to help them perform their jobs, fit for use and functioning every time. By recognizing that you have an obligation to your employees to develop vendors that consistently meet the employee's needs to do their jobs, it shows your employees they are important to you, and their end-customers.

Listen to your employees! Suppose you have a fleet of trucks and perform your own maintenance. Does it do any good to buy cheaper starter motors for your fleet vehicles if they have to be replaced twice as often? Are the mechanics the best decision makers, or someone sitting in an office? Viewed in this light, it becomes obvious that your suppliers affect your employees morale and job satisfaction. Employees do better work when they have what they need to do the job right. They want to be proud of their work, and they must have quality inputs to satisfy their customers, internal or external.

A world-class example is Xerox. One supplier says, "they tell you up front that you must produce perfect parts and how they'll work with you to reach that goal. If you're not ready for that commitment, you're wasting your time there." At Xerox, the employees help evaluate suppliers, and management respects and supports their recommendations.

Control for Outcomes, Not Decisions

Most managers have been trained in the fine art of controlling decisions. To become lean and mean, many companies are broadening managers' span of control. That means managers have less time to devote to each decision. This shift is forcing companies to examine how decisions get made in their organizations. Many are opting to control outcomes, leaving how the outcomes are achieved up to subordinates. Controlling for outcomes helps management have more control over its environment by being better informed and having more time to focus on those things it does particularly well. In addition, controlling outcomes is a built-in training mechanism for future managers in making their own decisions.

Implementing Quality: Lessons From The Pioneers

American companies are slowly, but surely, realizing that quality will soon be a competitive *necessity*, not a competitive weapon. Ken Albrecht writes in *Quality Digest* that there are five components to the paradigm shift from our old, introverted focus on processes, to an extroverted focus on customers that drive the quality process:

- From organizations that only produce . . . to organizations that perform.
- From structure . . . to culture.
- From control . . . to empowerment.
- From management . . . to leadership.

- From "quality" unto itself . . . to customer satisfaction.

How are companies making this paradigm shift and why is the success rate so low? Ernst & Young and the American Quality Foundation released their two year effort -- the *International Quality Study* -- that provides some answers. They analyzed 945 business practices of 584 companies from North America, Germany and Japan in manufacturing (autos and computer chips) and services (retail and banking) to find if there are any rules that should be followed in implementing a quality effort. The answer was a definite YES.

The study noted the success of each company's efforts depended on whether it was at the Novice, Journeyman or Master level at implementing quality. Some of the findings contradict conventional wisdom. For example, benchmarking of world-class companies was found to be useful only if the company already had a successful quality program — the Master level. Thus, if you attempt to emulate world-class practices, you will simply disrupt operations when you can't achieve the same results. Why? Without a quality culture, you won't be able to exploit the results of your benchmarking efforts.

Arthur D. Little Consultants surveyed 500 manufacturing and service companies using TQM, and found only 36% felt it was significantly boosting their competitiveness. Also in March, Rath & Strong Inc. asked 95 companies whether their TQM efforts had meet goals such as increased market share or customer satisfaction. More than half of the companies gave their efforts a D or F, and only 26% rated themselves an A or B.

The problem is not in the technique, but in the implementation. For small companies, it's mostly poor planning. Generally, it's a failure to link quality efforts with the bottom line. For example, if you start on team training, the yardstick should be the difference the training makes in performance -- not how many people went through the training.

How to begin? According to the International Quality Study (IQS), page 71, start by measuring your performance. The following chart lays out which "quality tools" to use at which stage of your quality trip. Clearly, not all quality efforts or techniques are beneficial to all companies. To find which level your company is at, compute two key measures: Return on Assets and Value Added per Employee. VAE is defined as sales less cost of goods sold, supplies and work done by outsiders. Do not subtract labor and administrative costs. Use the chart to determine at which of the three levels you are, and then learn from those that have gone before you.

International Quality Study

	NOVICE GETTING STARTED	JOURNEYMAN HONING SKILLS	MASTER STAYING ON TOP
ROA	Less than 2%	2% to 6.9%	7%+
Value Added Per Employee	Less than $47,000	$47,000 to $73,900	$74,000 and up
Employee Involvement	$$ Train heavily. Promote teamwork, but forget self-managed teams, which take heavy preparation. Limit employee empowerment to resolving customer complaints.	$$ Encourage employees at every level to find ways to do their jobs better -- and to simplify core operations. Set up a separate quality assurance staff.	$$ Use self-managed, multi-skilled teams that focus on horizontal processes such as logistics and product development. Limit training mainly to new hires.
Benchmarking	Emulate competitors, not world-class companies.	Imitate market leaders and selected world-class companies.	$$ Gauge product development, distribution, customer service vs. the best.
New Products	Rely mainly on customer input for ideas.	Use customer input, formal market research, and internal ideas.	Base on customer input, benchmarking, and internal R&D.
Supply Management	Choose suppliers mainly for price and reliability.	Select suppliers by quality certification, then price.	Choose suppliers mainly for their technology and quality.
New Technology	Focus on cost-reductions. Don't develop it -- buy it.	Find more flexible ways to use facilities to turn out a wider variety of products or services.	Use strategic partnerships to diversify manufacturer.

International Quality Study

	NOVICE GETTING STARTED	JOURNEYMAN HONING SKILLS	MASTER STAYING ON TOP
Manager / Employee Evaluation	Reward front-line workers for teamwork and quality.	Base compensation for workers and middle managers on contribution to teamwork and quality.	Include senior managers in compensation schemes pegged to teamwork and quality.
Quality Progress	$$ Concentrate on fundamentals. Identify processes that add value, simplify them, and move faster in response to customer and market demands. Don't bother using formal gauges of progress, gains will be apparent.	$$ Meticulously document gains and further refine practices to improve value added per employee, time to market and customer satisfaction.	Keep documenting gains and further refine practices to improve value added per employee, time to market and customer satisfaction.
$$ Areas where significant progress can be made.			

The IQS also noted that at U.S. companies, 29% evaluate the consequences of quality efforts less than once per year. Less than one-fourth translate customer expectations into new products or services. Only 22% use technology to meet customer expectations. And, 88% do not regularly use process improvement. Only 80% of U.S. companies regularly review quality performance, compared to 98% of Japanese companies — where 70% use quality information at least monthly.

Obviously, our use of quality information has a long way to go before it reaches parity with financial information. I hope we can afford the wait.

Everyone in the value chain — inside or outside the company — is a supplier or a customer. Japanese companies know precisely what they must demand from their suppliers, and therefore, what they must provide their customers. Japanese companies are committed to meeting the customer's needs every time -- not most of the time.

Many companies waste thousands, or even millions, of dollars on quality-improvement strategies that don't improve their performance and in fact, may be detrimental. Companies end up focusing on things that don't matter. To avoid wasted time and effort, first categorize each of your products/services into one of the quadrants on the grid.

Classifying your processes in this manner allows you to focus on what's important -- where to focus your dollars, time and energy to maximize your return on investment.

Quadrant I are products/services that your customers tell you they are not satisfied with, but product/service also isn't important. In other words, these don't contribute to your strategic mission, but your customers don't care. Get rid of these products/services.

Quadrant II are products/services that you're extremely good at (High Satisfaction), but customers don't care whether they buy from you (Low Importance). Many times, these products/services are commodities where a uniformly high level of satisfaction exists, but with comparable pricing, there's little to differentiate one vendor from another, so customers have little loyalty. These can be cash cows if you use the funds devoted to these products and services for Quadrant III.

Quadrant III products/services are of High Importance, but Low Satisfaction to your customers. Question: If these products/services are important to your customers, but they aren't happy, why are they buying from you? Answer: because you're the only game in town. If you don't protect your turf, somebody

Quadrant III	Quadrant IV
High Importance / Low Satisfaction	High Importance / High Satisfaction
These products/services must be moved to Quadrant IV to maintain competitive superiority.	Core Competency. Must do what ever it takes to maintain your market in these products/services.
Quadrant I	Quadrant II
Low Importance / Low Satisfaction	Low Importance / High Satisfaction
Customers aren't happy, but these products/services are not important. Get rid of them.	Products / services of high quality, but little importance buying from you. Cash cows (commodity).

will take this market niche away. You must move these products and services to Quadrant IV. Quadrant III items must be developed into core competencies if you're to fulfill your mission statement. But, where do you get the funds? From Quadrant II products and services. Understand this strategy means that you are "eating your own." You are making a conscience choice to get out of the Low Importance/High Satisfaction segment. Many times Quadrant III products and services are what the company was built on. Since then they have become a commodity. It's a tough decision. But, if you don't make it, your customers and competitors will.

Quadrant IV are your "core competencies" These must be maintained at all costs. These are the products and services that Xerox customers rate a "5". A core competence is looking at your company as a collection of the skills of your people, not your products or services.

Two examples. First, what products does Honda make? Among others: cars, motorcycles, snow blowers, outboard motors, generators. What do all these things have in common? Gasoline engines. Internally, Honda doesn't think of itself as a car or motorcycle company. Honda views itself as a collection of people that know how to generate power and transmit the power to do a job.

Second, when the cold war was winding down in the late 1980s, a ship building company wasn't getting many orders from the US Navy. So the CEO and President went to Europe looking for more business. In a hotel lobby, they had a chance encounter with the CEO of a German company. The German CEO asked what business the Americans were in. They replied, "We build ships for the Navy." The German CEO said, "No, that's not what I meant. How do you build the ships for the Navy?" The American CEO responded, "We buy these large plates of steel, cut them to size, bend them to shape, and drill holes in them. Then we weld all of them together, push the ship out on the water, and hope it doesn't sink." The German CEO said, "Oh, I see. You're in the business of designing and fabricating large complex metal structures." Get it?! Core competencies are the skills of your people, not the product you make or the service you provide.

What's the most reliable way to determine which quadrant each of your products/services fall into? How do you determine the Importance/Satisfaction of each service/product? Ask your customers. Unfortunately, customers will rarely offer you unbiased commentary. Most companies use an outside firm to undertake such a critical customer satisfaction survey. Don't make the mistake of conducting the survey yourself. No matter how hard you try, you will bias the results by asking only the questions that you know, and like, the answers to.

One of my clients had an excellent market research technique. Every time a potential customer called and was told the company did not have the product or service, the receptionists wrote it down. The owner figured the best market research in the world is people who are calling, checkbook in hand, ready to buy something. This captures buyers *behavior*, not just *attitude*, as surveys do.

To reiterate, a lot of money and time is spent on very broad quality efforts that don't work. Instead, take one small step at a time. This allows quick successes that can lay the groundwork for the really big changes you're looking for. Start with a few, highly focused practices and add more sophisticated ones later. For example, as noted in the IQS table above, lower performing companies usually don't have the training or strategy in place to use extensive "empowerment" of lower level employees. The corporate culture won't support it. You might start by giving customer representatives more authority to resolve customer complaints.

However, there are several techniques, almost cost free, that can be utilized by all companies. Explain your mission and strategic plan to all employees, customers and vendors, then create nonfinancial performance measures to tell whether you are meeting your mission and strategies; improve and simplify production and your product or service development process; and focus on shortening your "total cycle time." Joshua Hammond, the quality foundation's president was quoted as saying "The most popularly used practices are least effective, and the most effective practices are least used."

Is Empowerment Right for Your Organization?[4]

Empowerment of workers is "the" buzzword these days. However, empowerment works only in the right situation and environment, with the cooperation of management and employees. Give yourself the points of the answer you choose.

A. What is your organization's niche?

1. We are a low-cost, high-volume producer of a few commodities.

2. We produce a number of high-volume products for a few customers.

3. We produce a few products for "niche" markets.

4. We provide personalized products, tailored to each customer.

B. Are your employees ready for greater authority?

---

[4] Adapted from *Spirit,* Southwest Airlines, 1993, Chaudron Associates.

1. Our employees are not interested in having greater authority or responsibility.

2. A few employees want greater authority in doing their jobs.

3. A significant number of our employees want greater authority in doing their jobs.

4. Most employees are champing at the bit to have greater authority.

C. How much time do your employees spend with a customer?

1. They spend, at most, a few minutes with each customer.

2. They spend a few hours with each customer.

3. They spend days or weeks with each customer.

4. They spend months or years with each customer.

D. What is your business relationship with your customers?

1. We have a mechanical, distant relationship with our customers.

2. We try to minimize the time spent with customers.

3. We occasionally have social contact with our customers.

4. We try to create long-term friendships with our customers.

E. How easy is it to learn job knowledge?

1. It can be learned in a few short hours.

2. It takes a few days or months to learn.

3. It takes a few years to learn.

4. It takes a lifetime of learning.

F. How much does your business environment change?

1. Our business is relatively stable and unchanging.

2. We can accurately predict the changes that will occur.

3. We know only the outlines of changes that will affect us.

4. Our business environment changes from moment to moment, making employees react quickly.

G. What are your management's beliefs about employee motivation?

1. Management believes in manipulating people to think they have power.

2. Few in management believe employees have high needs for growth and success.

3. Some in management believe employees have high needs for growth and success.

4. Most, or all, management believe employees have high needs for growth and success.

H. Are your procedures fixed and stable?

1. We have a fixed, stable procedure for doing almost everything.

2. We have a set of procedures that covers much of what we do.

3. We have procedures on a few tasks.

4. We have no procedures because they wouldn't allow employees to make split-second decisions.

I. Is management ready to give greater authority?

1. It would be like pulling teeth for them to give up power.

2. A few would be willing to give authority to employees.

3. Many would be willing to give authority to employees.

4. Most, if not all, of management is willing to give authority.

Your Score:

28-36 points: Your organization probably is well suited and willing to give greater authority and responsibility to its employees. Employees and management need to clearly define their mutual expectations.

19-27 points: Your organization presents a "mixed bag" regarding empowerment. There should be serious discussion between management and employees on the need for empowerment.

9-18 points: Employee empowerment is probably not appropriate to your organization. Substantial changes might have to be made before significant employee empowerment occurs.

If you are ready for an empowered work force, the section on self-directed work teams might be just what you are looking for.

Speed to Market Requires Speedy Decisions...
In the 1970s, it was cost control. In the 1980s, it was quality. Now, those strategies are givens for world-class companies. Time-to-market is the competitive strategy for the 1990s. Time-to-market begins with how management makes decisions, how information and data are accumulated and processed. I recently read somewhere that for every person that is added to the decision making process, the time to make a decision doubles.

Question: Can management learn to make faster and better decisions? Answer: Yes. How? Kathleen M. Eisenhardt studied 12 micro-computer companies. As reported in *California Management Review*, the successful companies had distinct differences in their decision making processes. Fast Decision Makers decide on critical issues within two to four months such as product innovations, strategic alliances and redirection. Slow Decision Makers take 12 to 18 months to make similar decisions. The results of the study run counter to what many of us, with financial backgrounds, have come to consider gospel. But, there is something to be learned here.

The decision making processes of the 12 firms were tracked and analyzed with extensive interviews with each member of top management. In addition, questionnaires were completed and group meetings were observed. The authors made numerous contacts with key executives of comparable outside firms to confirm their in-house findings.

The Myths of Conventional Wisdom At first, conventional wisdom appears to accelerate decisions. But, these myths ignore the realities decision makers must face.

Myth #1 Skimp on analysis by looking at limited amounts of information. Consider only one or two alternatives. Issue: Does management have enough information to make a quality decision?

Myth #2 Limit conflict. It drags out decisions. Issues: Can quality decisions be made without conflict? Will managers who are ignored support the decision?

Myth #3 Be autocratic, a swashbuckler, make unilateral decisions. Issues: Does the autocratic manager know enough to be effective? Will uninvolved managers/personnel support and enthusiastically implement decisions they don't "own"?

The Fast Decision Maker: Several issues were found to be critical to an understanding of how Fast Decision Makers made successful decisions (in terms of their companies' success). How do Fast Decision Makers accelerate efficient use of information? Are there ways to deal with the anxiety of rapid decision making in a highly uncertain environment? Can groups build equity into the decision making process? Yes.

Fast Decision Makers use simple, but powerful tools to monitor real-time operating information and utilize fast, comparative analysis of multiple alternatives. Fast Decision Makers use rapid conflict resolution to maintain cohesive decision making groups. Fast Decision Makers seek out trusted advisors and use confidence building techniques. Slow Decision Makers get mired in endless searches for more information, development of alternatives and exhibit an inability to resolve conflict.

More Information — Not Less Rather than limiting the amount of analysis, Fast Decision Makers generally consider as much, if not more, information than their slower counterparts, but completely different kinds of information. Slow Decision Makers rely on formal planning and futuristic information to track possible technological paths, markets, and competitor actions. All of which is extremely time consuming. Fast Decision Makers utilize real-time information about current operations that can be reported with little time lag.

For quantitative data, Fast Decision Makers monitor a wide variety of internal operating performance measures as their most critical information resource, some on a daily basis. Fast Decision Makers look at orders, backlog, margins, engineering milestones, cash, scrap rates, and work-in-process — real-time information. Slow Decision Makers prefer the more refined accounting based measures like profitability — old, late, out of date, information.

You might think the finance executive in an operationally focused environment might be shoved aside. Not so. Because Fast Decision Makers need rapid information with a high degree of reliability, they utilize the finance executive to provide the "pulse" of the organization. Therefore, the financial executive must stay close to operations.

Fast Decision Makers also use frequent meetings to deal with the less quantifiable operational data. Such meetings have an urgency attached to them to cover "what's happening" throughout the organization. Such meetings tend to be emotional, intense, and vocal. Slow Decision Makers, on the other hand, tend to have fewer operational meetings, and focus on future, not current, information using memos rather than face-to-face meetings.

Fast Decision Makers tend to take on duties out of their traditional roles. For example, the VP of Marketing might track competitor moves (e.g., new product introductions) requiring frequent phone calls and travel. The VP of R&D might maintain contact with leading universities to stay abreast of current technological developments.

Real-time information speeds decision making because managers can spot opportunities and problems earlier. Real-time information becomes your early warning system. When a problem occurs, you don't waste time searching for the relevant information.

Emerging research suggests that intuition is primarily based on experience. Intuitive managers learn to process information in "blocks," and thus, can process information much faster than laymen. This explains why many firms that are described as "laid-back" and simply "have a feeling for the market" are, in fact, developing their "intuition" by tracking real-time information. In the study, the executives who used the most real-time information also were described as the most intuitive.

One extremely interesting finding was that Fast Decision Makers regard long-term, formal, planning as a waste of time. Why? It's difficult to predict what will happen and impossible to predict who will do what and when. As one Fast Decision Maker claimed, "No company can know how things will evolve. You can only monitor the outside world and direct the evolving strategy that you see. Overall, it appears that real-time information — which gives executives an intimate knowledge of their business speeds choice, but planning information — which attempts to predict the future — does not."

Fewer Alternatives   At first, logic would have it that the fewer alternatives there are to analyze, the faster the decisions can be made. However, Fast Decision Makers do the opposite. Fast Decision Makers seek out and debate multiple alternatives. Sometimes, to foster debate, Fast Decision Makers will throw out an alternative they do not support. The idea that this approach is ambiguous and complicated is precisely the point. It stretches you, as a manager, to think in a non-sequential manner, which is exactly the way the market works; in leaps and bounds, not in a smooth, orderly, sequential, manner that our planning systems present.

But why are multiple alternatives faster than the sequential approach we learned and use? Answer — Comparison. The ability to play one alternative against another sharpens your preferences. An example: Looking for a new car? Is it easier to decide if you look at ads in the classifieds, or if you go for test drives? Test drives allow you to rank your preferences of the alternatives, even if you can't quantify the alternatives.

More explicitly, assume you are from Mars, land on earth, and have never seen a car before, let alone driven one. Now, I meet you in the parking lot with a Ford Escort, take you for a drive around the parking lot, and then ask you to rank the Escort on a scale of 1 to 10. Easy or hard? Hard. You have no basis of comparison. No frame of reference.

Now I drive you around in a Lincoln Mark VI, and ask you to tell me which you like better, the Escort or the Mark VI. Easier or more difficult? Easier. Why? You have a frame of reference. One car against the other. Classified ads are abstract. The Fast Decision Makers would say the ads are "planning," versus test drives, which are "real-time information," which monitor the market.

No company can know how things will evolve. You can only monitor the outside world and direct the evolving strategy that you see.

Fast Decision Makers reported that analyzing multiple alternatives builds confidence because it develops a feeling that a superior alternative wasn't overlooked. You probably would not buy a car without seeing and test driving others because you would wonder if you missed something better.

How are Fast Decision Makers and Slow Decision Makers fundamentally different? Fast Decision Makers rapidly analyze multiple alternatives relying on quick, comparative analysis to reveal relative preferences without the need for absolute quantification. Fast Decision Makers like "breadth — not depth." On the other hand, Slow Decision Makers rely on in-depth analysis to quantify a few alternatives which, unfortunately, does not result in the same confidence.

Use a Counselor   It was found that Fast Decision Makers rely on a two-tier system of advice wherein all executives offer advice, but the decision maker places particular reliance on "counselors," the most experienced executives. Counselors work in the background, acting as a confidential sounding board on a wide range of ideas. Slow Decision Makers generally don't develop counselors on which they rely.

What is the profile of counselors? They are consistently older, highly experienced, considered savvy or street smart, and have given up the career chase to the top. Counselors replace their ride on the fast track to the top with the personal challenge inherent in being a counselor. What did Fast Decision Makers do when no counselor was available within the company? One firm hired a consultant who had been a senior executive at two leading firms in the industry.

How do counselors accelerate decisions? First, they provide high-quality advice by assessing situations more rapidly. Second, counselors understand discretion and the subtle exercise of power. Third, when the stakes are high and the uncertainties large, counselors reduce the decision maker's anxiety, which increases confidence, leading to faster decisions. Thus, counselors counteract the tendency to procrastinate

Conflict -- Harmful or Helpful? Obviously, conflict can paralyze decision making. But, Fast Decision Makers use a two-tier technique to manage conflict, termed by one Fast Decision Maker as "consensus with qualification," to resolve deadlocks. First, Fast Decision Makers cover an issue with all affected managers to gain consensus. If agreement cannot be reached, the key executive and the most relevant functional manager make the decision explicitly taking into consideration input from all affected managers.

Slow Decision Makers, on the other hand, often wait for a deadline to force a decision or wait extended periods for consensus. Slow Decision Makers sometimes rationalize their indecision by continual refining of their proposal in hopes that the management team will accept the plan. Waiting for complete agreement usually means that no decision will be made since it gives everyone veto power and nothing gets accomplished.

How does consensus with qualification accelerate decisions? It recognizes that conflict in decision making is natural, productive, and inevitable. To be effective, managers must make choices even when there is disagreement. And, affected managers like the consensus methodology for two reasons. First, everyone accepts that their opinion may not always be the one adopted, but everyone likes to be heard. Second, it gives managers an added influence when the decision significantly affects their part of the organization.

Active Coping   Fast Decision Makers generally don't know it, but they are using "active coping" to deal with high anxiety decisions. Active coping simply means Fast Decision Makers are proactive and structure their behavior to deal with situations where the information is poor and the stakes are high. Fast Decision Makers take concrete steps to enhance their feelings of competence. Control boosts their confidence to make tough decisions.

Fast Decision Makers also see each decision as an integral part of a whole. Slow Decision Makers see each decision as a separate and distinct event, which heightens their anxiety worse because decisions remain abstract, unattached to other activities. One Slow Decision Maker summed it up this way: "Over the years it had become obvious that I didn't know any more even though I waited."

Conclusion Time-to-market has emerged as a critical competitive weapon. Time-to-market requires fast decisions. For most decision makers, simply speeding up their current style will not work. Many will have to adopt a different philosophy such as the one discussed here. In the study, Fast Decision Makers linked the speed of their strategic decisions with their companies' success. They commented: "you have to keep up with the train;" "you've got to catch the high opportunities;" "simply do something;" etc. For the most part, Slow Decision Makers managed poor performing companies, some of which failed. They missed opportunities.

Fast decisions in five easy steps:
1. Track real-time-information to develop your "intuition." Focus on operating performance measures and critical environmental factors.
2. Use multiple alternatives for comparison, eliminating the need for quantification.
3. Get everyone's advice, but rely on your trusted counselors.
4. Try for agreement. Involve everyone in the decision, but don't delay. Make the decision in conjunction with those most affected. Delay won't make you popular.
5. View your decision as part of a larger whole to avoid mismatched decisions in the future.

Measuring the RIGHT Performance for Competitive Superiority

Prof. Joseph Fisher[5] studied the use of operational performance measures to achieve Competitive Superiority in 5 successful high tech manufacturing companies. This excellent overview shows why we must get back to basics, so our work force can understand and act to satisfy customers.

The companies were "shocked" into examining their management control systems: loss of a significant customer,

---

[5] "Use of Nonfinancial Performance Measures," *The Journal of Cost Management*, Spring 1992, pg. 31, Joseph Fisher, Assistant Professor of Business, Amos Tuck School of Management, Dartmouth College, now at University of Indiana.

moving the plant, increased competition. Such shocks made it clear that it no longer was business as usual. A whole new philosophy and management structure had to be devised. Why? Management found Traditional Financial Measurements to be inadequate in their rapidly changing environment, where the product life cycle is, at most, 18 months.

Why don't Traditional Performance Measures work in a dynamic environment? Business is like a baseball game. You can't win the game by watching the scoreboard (Traditional Performance Measures). You can only win the game by keeping your eye on the ball (Operational Performance Measures). The scoreboard tells you only the result of your efforts, it doesn't show you how you're hitting, catching, fielding, or pitching.

Why financial measures don't work   All of the companies had used a traditional variance system built on a standard cost system that wasn't getting the job done. Here's why:

Actionability   The companies' operating departments felt the variance system produced information that was useful only to the "bean counters." People on the shop floor couldn't understand the data, let alone act on it. Data was so summarized that managers didn't see a direct connection between their actions on the floor and the information in "their" reports. Result — no one takes responsibility and variance reports are ignored. Example: machine hour variances which indicate if a machine is being used efficiently, but does nothing to point out the cause(s) of, or solution to, the variance.

Inadequate overhead allocations All the firms discovered that allocating overhead based on machine or labor hours was disfunctional. Overhead almost never behaves in direct proportion to changes in these hours. Most firms were implementing activity-based costing to address this problem.

Conflicts Managers whose compensation is based on variances will engage in goal discongruity; that is, they will maximize their own compensation to the detriment of the company. For example, a purchasing manager may buy cheaper raw materials to get a bigger paycheck, causing manufacturing to have a negative variance due to low quality inputs. Another example is the plant manager, knowing standard cost includes a fixed component, manufactures unneeded products to soak up negative variances caused by idle capacity. The resulting finished product then has to be written off as obsolete.

To be useful in a highly dynamic environment, standard costs need to be updated instantly and constantly. Since that is not possible, the shop floor considers the data out of date and useless. Usually at least 30 days old by the time it's received, the information is of little practical use to the machine operator.

Further, the standards themselves and the standard setting process conflict with continuous improvement by setting a goal of "good enough," rather than motivating an attitude of constant improvement. Standards set by management act as an upper boundary, limiting performance. Workers often feel if they ever make the mistake of attaining the standard, management will raise it, without raising pay.

Operational Performance Measures: Doing It Right   Many firms are reevaluating their reason for being in business and conclude they are not in business to make a profit, but profit is the result of satisfying customers. Refocusing requires the following:

Key Success Factors   Decide how you're going to succeed in the marketplace. What drives your company: customer satisfaction, manufacturing excellence, market leadership, quality, reliability, responsiveness, technology leadership, superior financial results? Note: Since most key success factors do not rely on cost considerations, standard cost systems are inadequate to control the company.

Measuring Key Success Factors is much more difficult than it appears. For example: If you want to measure your on-time delivery performance, simply compute the percent of products going out the door as promised. But, if you measure or compensate employees on such a system, they will quickly figure out how to beat the system. How? Consider: You have two shipments, one is already late, and the other will be timely only if it goes first. So, you put the employees in the position of 100% of the shipments being late if they are handled in sequential order. The system is *goal discongruent*. What the employees will figure out in short order is to ship the second order first and on-time, making the first shipment really late, resulting in only a 50% late score. Which do you think the employees will do? The second. The employees will *game* the system to their advantage. The solution? Age the shipments, just like you age accounts receivable. This results in the desired behavior being rewarded.

Measuring on-time shipments (when the order was shipped) is better than no measurement. But, does your customer care when the order was shipped? No. Your customer cares only whether the order was received on time. On-time *shipments* is an *internal* focus. Measuring on-time *deliveries* is an *external* focus.

The Major Problem If you adopt the aging schedule and employees behave appropriately, the question is "What is the benefit to the bottom line?" Unfortunately, a way has not been found to directly track the financial benefit of improved customer service.

You will confront several major issues in adopting Operational Performance Measures:
1. Determining acceptable operational performance measures;
2. Determining who is responsible for which Operational Performance Measures and;
3. What constitutes effective performance?

Achieving continuous improvement Fisher discovered several approaches to continuous improvement. The most efficient seemed to be to use the prior period's actual performance as the benchmark. Since the target is always moving, current period performance equal to the prior period is unacceptable.

Problem solving Companies use two approaches. First, form committees consisting of senior managers and others familiar with the specific area to tackle each key success factor. The team would: determine how to measure performance; collect data to find the source of failure; test possible corrective actions, selecting the best solution; and develop an implementation plan. The second approach involved delegating the

responsibility to the department that has the majority of influence:
- Manufacturing department control based on cycle times;
- Production planning department control using on-time deliveries and inventory levels;
- Quality Control based on customer returns.

Benefits/Detriments of Operational Performance Measures
The studied firms noted Operational Performance Measures were more directly tied to the key success factors, possibly because they do not require "dollarizing." Thus, Operational Performance Measures are "actionable" at the operating level — workers don't have to be accountants to understand the information at which they are looking. And, Operational Performance Measures are available much more quickly to those who need the information to run their operation. A drop in quality could be quickly identified and corrected. Operational Performance Measures can also identify problems that Traditional Performance Measures cannot, such as poor customer response time. Traditional Performance Measures simply tell you the result, in dollars, but not the cause of problems.

On the downside, the inability to dollarize the profitability of the improvement in Operational Performance Measures leaves managers who are still rewarded purely on Traditional Performance Measures in an awkward position. For example, a traditional accounting system does not capture the lost revenue due to poor on-time performance. Or, consider when new equipment is purchased to shorten order times. If the unit is a profit center, the costs incurred are directly traceable to the income statement, but the increased revenue probably is not.

The use of operational performance measures for organizational control is in its infancy. For many managers, it requires a leap of faith to adopt Operational Performance Measures and hope that the bottom line shows results. Many world-class companies are making the leap. Can you?

Activity vs. Results: Most companies are relatively good at setting the goals that need to be achieved. But, many times things get muddled in translating the goals into the actions needed to accomplish the goal. For example, management wants the sales department to generate 5% "new business" this year. The Sales VP agrees what constitutes "new business," calls a meeting of the sales staff, and a plan is mapped out to increase the number of calls made. Each sales person is to make an additional 10 calls per day. Unfortunately, the last step results in a change of focus from results (new business) to activity (calls). The next question should be "How many calls, to whom, how often, and, is there a premium for new business?." If the last action steps are left out, the sales staff will lose sight of the reason for the activity.

Well defined goals are (1) specific, (2) attainable, (3) measurable, and (4) in a specific time frame. "I want to save the down payment for a house" is not an effective goal statement. A New Years' resolution of "I want to save $100 per week this year to buy a house next February" is a well defined goal. It is specific ($100 per week), attainable (or the commitment wouldn't be made), measurable ($50 per week is not $100) and has a deadline.

Benchmarking: THE Tool to Beat Your Competitors' Brains Out

What is benchmarking? There are as many definitions as there are benchmarking consultants. David Kearns, retired CEO at Xerox Corporation, who led his company to the Malcolm Baldrige National Quality Award in 1989, defined benchmarking as ". . .the continuous process of measuring your products, services, and practices against your toughest competitors or those organizations recognized as leaders." Benchmarking is the number one reengineering technique because it is quantifiable.

Benchmarking, or competitive benchmarking as it is sometimes known, is a process developed initially in manufacturing organizations, such as Xerox. When it was primarily a manufacturing-based process, it was more commonly performed as competitive benchmarking. Benchmarking started in manufacturing because of global competition. Techniques have now been developed for virtually all service businesses and support or administrative areas. In fact, benchmarking actually works best in small firms which have fewer layers of management.

Competitive benchmarking stacks your company up against a direct industry competitor. However, in recent years, with an increasing emphasis on the development and implementation of quality strategies, the use of benchmarking has been expanded to include administration, customer service, and sales operations. The table, Nonmanufacturing Areas to Benchmark, can be of help:

Nonmanufacturing Areas to Benchmark

Customer Satisfaction	Business Results	Employee Satisfaction
Customer requirements	Local market segmentation	Hiring practices
Order-to-install processes	Most successful competitor	Org. structure / response
Problem-resolution	Local advertising	Org. structure / response
Post-sale customer support	Paperwork practices	Manpower requirements
Telephone answering	Parts/supplies inventory Sales productivity Service productivity	Recog/reward programs Empowerment Training Advancement policies

Two other approaches that may be more effectively implemented are *functional* and *internal* benchmarking. Although functional benchmarking may be done within your own industry, it could be a completely different industry. The focus of benchmarking is on a specific functional process or business practice. For example, Xerox benchmarked its distribution function against L.L. Bean. Flannel shirts don't have anything to do with parts for photocopiers, but that's not the comparison. The comparison is the process of running a warehouse. L.L. Bean is renowned as the best in distribution efficiency and customer service.

How do you think the copier parts were stored on the shelves in a Xerox warehouse? In part number order, of course. Why? For whose benefit are the parts stored in part number order? For the accounting department, because the accountants have to take inventory *once* each year. So, we make the warehouse employees work in a dysfunctional system all year, because accountants have to take inventory.

How do you think L.L. Bean arranges its goods on the shelves? In picking order. The most frequently picked (i.e., highest volume) items are stocked at the front of the warehouse, nearest the picking station. This minimizes the number of steps, and time, it takes to pull the ordered items off the shelves. When do you think the flannel shirts are near the picking station? Fall and winter. Where are they in the spring and summer? In the back of the warehouse. It's OK to move the inventory around. If you make the warehouse workers jobs easier, they will figure out where the stock is. Better yet, since the warehouse employees have to work under a system, why not let them decide how to arrange the inventory?

Letting the accounting department decide how to store the inventory in the warehouse is like the proverbial "tail wagging the dog." Other than for internal controls, the accounting department should rarely be able to dictate operations.

Internal benchmarking capitalizes on what Tom Peters refers to as "pockets of excellence." This is where an organizational unit with superior performance becomes the benchmark for other similar units. Internal benchmarking can be useful in process improvement where there is significant variation between a best performing unit and others. The goal is to capture the benefits that led to the unit's superior performance.

The Pioneers In the early 1980s, Xerox Corporation pioneered the use of benchmarking. Why was Xerox attracted to benchmarking long before the quality movement got under way in the U.S.? Because as late as 1975, Xerox had more than 90% of the market share for copiers in the United States. However, by 1980, Japanese competitors had captured 40% of the U.S. market. Benchmarking, coupled with employee involvement, was initially the centerpiece of what later became Leadership Through Quality — Xerox's name for its corporate quality strategy. In the beginning, the objective of benchmarking was to develop a more competitive product line to halt the rapid erosion of market share.

As an example, the Xerox 1075 copier/duplicator was highly acclaimed in the U.S. But the acid test came in Japan, where the 1075 became the first foreign product to win Japan's Grand Design Prize for Engineering. Xerox is recognized as perhaps the only major American firm to regain significant market share that was previously lost to foreign competition.

The Ford Taurus is another example of product development through the application of benchmarking. In the early 1980s, Donald Peterson, then CEO of Ford Motor Company, assembled a product development team to examine competitive automobiles from around the world to incorporate their best features into the then new Taurus. In other words, what were the product attributes that resulted in customers buying a particular model? In this way, no single competitive product was selected as the best one. A Swedish car may have been the benchmark for seats; a Japanese model may have become the benchmark for paint, and so on. More than 500 component areas were isolated for analysis.

Peterson's objective was to "better the best" in as many of the areas as possible. The product development team was able to improve upon the competition in 350, or 70%, of the 500 components. The Taurus became a top selling automobile and led the turnaround at Ford.

Benchmarking in Smaller Companies   Although Xerox, Ford and other large corporations pioneered benchmarking, you don't have to be a big company to take advantage of the power of this technique. Today, smaller and mid-sized firms are discovering that they too can seize the high-leverage power of benchmarking. For example, Atlanta-based Risk Sciences Group, Inc., a $2.6 million (revenue) insurance firm, used benchmarking to gain better cost control and to provide its clients world-class quality service at competitive prices.

Getting Started Top management must not only be supportive of the effort, but more importantly, they must provide leadership to achieve the full advantage of benchmarking as a high-leverage tool for positive change. This does not mean top management should commission the process and force it upon the organization.

Management must learn enough about empowerment to know that the effectiveness of a management tool, such as benchmarking, is highly dependent on how it is developed and implemented within the context of a specific organization and its culture. To achieve the greatest synergy, cross-functional teams should be developed. Team membership should include those whose organizational units and business processes will be affected by the change process.

The benchmarking process consists of four phases: planning, analysis, integration, and implementation. To ensure success, it's important that the process be developed with this sequence, and that the team clearly understands the following: the organizational process being improved, the performance of the benchmark, the size of the performance gap, and the key causes for the gap. Only then can effective actions be taken to improve the operation.

Planning   Do you know where you are now? The first step in benchmarking is to identify what is to be benchmarked, i.e., what in your operation may be an opportunity for improvement? Concentrate on organizational outputs. This will afford the greatest opportunity for sustainable results.

Avoid trying to do too much at once. An entire organization cannot be benchmarked because it would be too complex, especially for a beginner. Start with one process or in one functional area, and after learning and applying your new found knowledge, move into other areas. This is a continuous improvement process! Internal reviews of operations will identify some possibilities, but don't forget to go to the real source. Ask your customers what is important and what they would like to see you change.

Key customers should participant in the improvement process. They can provide crucial information inputs and assure greater success. For example, if a key customer would like to see you improve your level of customer service, invite them to participate on the benchmarking team to improve it. They can help you develop operational definitions, select key measurements, etc. This way you have direct market input to your new process that will make it much more relevant.

Before You Benchmark. . .

Eighty percent of companies fail to achieve the potential that benchmarking offers. Fifty percent have a negative experience that can stymie the effort to improve. Dan Ciampa, CEO of Rath and Strong, Lexington, Massachusetts, offers these tips:

Benchmarking best practices. As opposed to traditional benchmarking, which focuses on strategic information, such as revenue per employee, "best-practices" benchmarking illustrates how well you perform a task compared to highly efficient companies. Best-practices benchmarking works by exposing employees on how to better do their jobs.

Structure benchmarking to maximize employee learning. Don't hire outside consultants to visit other companies and report back. Send employee teams, making certain to include those who will be responsible for implementing the changes. In addition, require a formal, written report and make it clear that the team will have to teach others in the company that could benefit from the information.

Use "break through" teams. Select people who are excited about the prospect of change and the challenge of doing their jobs better. This is not the time to try and open the eyes of stubborn employees.

Preparation. Ask the benchmarking team to determine which areas it would like to improve, then they're committed. This will create a willingness to learn, and the team members will ask meaningful questions.

Implementing productivity programs in financial management areas has proven difficult. The project involves "benchmarking" and "best practices."

Benchmarking will provide critical information for organizations seeking to improve their financial productivity. Under an agreement with the AICPA, the Hackett Group, a Cleveland management consulting firm, will conduct a project to provide critical information for organizations seeking to improve the productivity of their financial areas.

The Hackett Group will expand its existing data base to contain extensive information from corporations and government entities about key management accounting practices. The best-run companies identify their practices. Management receives a confidential performance analysis to compare aspects of their company's accounting functions to benchmarks developed from the data base. In turn, the AICPA will inform the financial community of the "best practices" identified in the study.

The Management Accounting Executive Committee of the Institute is overseeing the study and will publish the results of the project to the membership. For more information, call John Morrow at the Institute at 201-938-3011.[6]

The American Productivity & Quality Center has established the International Benchmarking Clearinghouse. The Clearinghouse offers the opportunity to learn what sets top performing companies above the rest. It helps you implement that learning. The Clearinghouse was designed with the ideas and active involvement of 87 organizations that participated in the *Design Steering Committee.* These are the major reasons the Clearinghouse was created:

1. Simplify access to benchmark information.
2. Broaden and increase ease of networking.
3. Save significant time and cost.

---

[6] "Benchmarking Information: Where to Find It," *The CPA Letter,* April 1993, American Institute of CPAs, New York, NY.

4. Improve the quality of benchmark information.
5. Improve internal benchmark processes.
6. Stimulate action and continuous improvement.
7. Provide knowledge/support for Malcolm Baldrige National Quality Award applicants.
8. Demonstrate corporate leadership.

Fees: a one-time initiation fee, based on the number of employees, ranges from $3,000 to $12,000 for Basic Services plus Networking. An annual fee per participant from $6,000 for the first employee participant, declining to $4,200 per participant for 21+. If you need only the Basic services, not the Network, the first participant is $2,000 and declining to $1,400 for 21+.

Reengineering: Internal or External?

Most reengineering efforts focus on internal processes, without first asking what the customer wants. This is one reason why so many profit improvement efforts fail. Companies improve processes that customers place only marginal value on. Customer benchmarking overcomes the shortcomings of looking at internal processes without regard to whether or not improvements improve customer profitability.

A crucial point should be understood early in the benchmarking process. You should clearly understand your own process before you set out to benchmark a superior performer. If you are standing still .... you are going backwards. Your customers don't judge you in a vacuum. They judge you relative to your competition. If you are standing still, and your competitors are moving forward to provide better service or products — to your customers it appears you are going backwards.

The business arena is a more dynamic environment than sports. Nothing stays the same for very long. So, as improvement trends are extended over future periods, be sure to extrapolate where the benchmark will be moving to and at what rate of improvement.

Gain commitment   Up to this point, no behavioral change has been made in how work is done. You should have a clear understanding of the current process. A benchmark performance gap has been identified. Cause and effect analyses should focus on reasons why the gap exists. This is a learning process and an understanding should be starting to emerge. Typically, some participants will resist initial findings. Care should be taken to avoid creating feelings of recrimination and defensiveness. Your primary objective is to improve. New information will point out where you have opportunities for improvement. However, how you react to this new information will have a strong influence on your success in changing your performance. The first reaction of many is denial. The data must be wrong.

Prior to actual implementation - where action plans will be developed and implemented - findings should be communicated to the team players. This task will be much easier if the organization has already achieved a high level of trust developed through participation and involvement. As was discussed earlier, cross-functional teams of those who will be affected by the change process should be active participants in benchmarking. This will ensure consensus and commitment because the employees will be implementing *their* action plans, not someone else's.

Just do it! The Nike slogan — "Just do it!" — has become popular. Our culture seems to place an inordinate value on action itself. However, no action should be taken before its time. The planning and analysis points us to what actions are needed and where to make changes to achieve your improvement goals. The integration phase ensures everyone understands and is committed to the change process and to the specific changes agreed upon to bring about your objectives. The development and implementation of action plans, the monitoring of progress, and the recalibration of benchmark indices can be done with a higher probability of success.

Having completed your homework of what to do and where to do it, now it's time to determine the "how" of process improvement. Functional action plans should address assignment responsibility, specific task requirements, resource requirements, and define expected results. Plans in this phase must be operationalized. They must become integrated into the action orientation of the entire organization. Outcomes of the changes must be monitored to ascertain effectiveness in achieving stated goals and to allow for necessary corrective action.

Finally, after the benchmarking process has run its full course and improvement goals have been attained, you must recalibrate your benchmark standards. The analogy here is like a ratchet. The first cycle brings up improvement and you raise your performance to the benchmark level. Then start at the beginning and repeat the process. Remember, champions continuously strive for improvement and always seek to break the old performance records.

Benchmarking: What it is not Benchmarking should not be seen as a turnaround strategy. If a firm is failing, it is usually too late to marshal the necessary energy and resources in time for these techniques to work. Benchmarking is a long-term technique for continuous improvement. The companies who best implement benchmarking are those willing to explore what at first may seem like strange new lands. And, superior companies stay out front by continually working to become better by using high-leverage techniques such as benchmarking.

While benchmarking is a high-leverage tool for improvement, it is not a quick fix. It requires commitment by management and extensive training for successful implementation. There will be a unique learning curve associated with your specific business. Your organization's prior work and experience in quality improvement will be a factor in the shape of the learning curve, as well as the rate at which you will be able move along the curve.

Benchmarking is *not the solution*; it's the *tool* to enable the solution. As is the case with most tools, benchmarking tools often are best used in conjunction with other tools. For example, another management technique receiving much attention today is self-directed work teams. Highly autonomous teams provide an environment and culture that is more conducive to the implementation of process improvements resulting from benchmarking. I've included a separate section on self-directed work teams.

The Big Picture: Systems thinking - inputs and outputs
Whether your firm's primary strategy is cost leadership, differentiation, or carving out a specialized niche, benchmarking can be an effective tool to analyze your company's situation within the strategic planning process. A systems focus on your process, and its inputs and outputs, can aid in understanding the total organization and the cause and effect relationships that exist at various critical points. For example, a manufacturing firm can use benchmarking to study the activity-cost chain. Start internally and move into forward channel activities, such as the wholesale and retail distribution functions, to see the affects on those outputs as your product or service moves along the supply chain to the ultimate customer.

This process also can be performed backward into supplier-related activities that are inputs to your production or service processes. Building and maintaining rapport with suppliers is critical to the success of a manufacturer. Problems brought into the production process from an outside supplier will move through your process chain to the customer. The customer will never blame a supplier for the failure of your product or service. In the eyes of your customer, it was your product or service that failed. Quality-oriented companies understand they are an integral part of this chain. This would be an appropriate place to start working on supplier-vendor partnerships. It could be another opportunity to benchmark!

Creating Windows: Focusing on the external environment
The organization can become a distraction to your real purpose. It's easy to get bogged down internally. Xerox's management discovered this in 1980 when they finally realized that the Japanese had eaten their lunch and were sitting down to dinner! The Japanese were selling copiers that equaled or exceeded Xerox's quality - at a price less than Xerox's production cost! The organization is created as a vehicle, or means, to accomplish your goals and objectives, to achieve your mission, and to move toward the realization of your vision.

The organization should not become an end in itself. Benchmarking can help to remove the blinders that keep us from seeing clearly what is in your environment, much of which can be detrimental to your continued success and even your survival. Consequently, benchmarking will broaden your view of the competitive arena, as well as, your scope of influence.

Benchmarking is a way to create windows to the external environment and your customers. In building feedback loops from your customers back into your organizational processes, feedback for continuous improvement is increased. The greater the feedback, the more you learn, and the larger the windows become, further expanding your learning process, much like concentric circles getting larger and larger. Benchmarking is a way for your company to become a learning organization that focuses on continuous improvement which leads to a position of leadership and superiority.

Benchmarking: 10 Reasons It Doesn't Work Benchmarking, if done correctly, constantly forces you to ask "Why?" But, to understand the answers you find by benchmarking, you MUST have a full grasp of your internal processes to compare with the data you'll gather from other companies. Digital Equipment has prepared the following list of the 10 Most Common Benchmarking Mistakes:

1. Your internal process is unexamined. You will waste your time gathering data if you have not compiled data on your processes with which to compare it.
2. Your site visits "feel good," but don't elicit data or ideas. To maximize the benefits of your effort, you must return with

hard, quantifiable data: percentage rework, total order cycle time, machine downtime, call-back rates, and abandon rates.
3. Your questions and goals are vague. Benchmarking is usually combined with other changes in your output stream, such as self-directed work teams. To focus their efforts and produce the maximum profit for the input, provide the teams with hard, quantifiable goals. How much do you expect the team to reduce rework? Tell them, then get out of the way. If you simply say, "reduce rework," the team will waste hours trying to decide "by how much."
4. Your effort is too broad or has too many parameters. Focus on a single or a few processes until you get the hang of benchmarking. You are doomed to failure if you try to benchmark an entire organization - it's too complex - you don't know what you're looking for. Even a department is too complex to benchmark. Instead of benchmarking the accounting department, tackle one process, such as accounts payable or customer billing.
5. Your focus is not on processes. Benchmarking is not competitive analysis, which only tells you "what" the differences are, but not "why" they exist. Benchmarking allows you to go "behind the scenes" to ferret out the reasons the differences exist.

6. Your benchmarking team is not committed to the effort. Without hard, quantifiable goals, the team has a difficult time determining what its mission is. It's difficult to be committed to something you can't identify. Another way to make certain people are not committed is to force them onto the benchmarking team. Do this, and they will sabotage the effort. Use volunteers, people who are excited and challenged by change.
7. You don't assign homework and/or advanced research to the benchmarking team. Such research provides a sense of urgency and concreteness so the benchmarking will be much more productive.
8. You select the wrong benchmark partner. Remember, it's your processes that you want to benchmark, not your product or services.
9. You fail to look outside your industry. Because you are benchmarking processes, the "best in class" is rarely in your industry.
10. You don't take any follow-up action. If you're not making progress, you're falling behind. Your competition will be moving forward while you are standing still. If the CEO, CFO, President or owner hands the benchmarking effort off to a mid-level manager, it sends the message the work is not important, and the rest of the company will ignore it.

Fire Your Customers

That's right, get rid of some of your customers. They aren't worth the effort. When times get tough, many companies institute price cuts to retain customers. In the short term, it's the easy thing to do. It's quick. It's easy. But, price cuts are usually a knee jerk reaction. Competing based on price is appropriate only if your product or service is truly a commodity and you have no way to differentiate it, and that's rarely the case. Virtually every product or service can be differentiated from the competition.

But, I would like you to think about whether all of your customers are worth the effort. Let's look at three reasons price reductions are usually the wrong strategy:

First, lowering prices will increase revenues. But, on average, a 20% revenue increase is needed to offset a 5% price reduction. Every dollar of a price cut is pure profit lost. But only a fraction of each new sales dollar goes to the bottom line. Do your own computation. Can you increase revenues enough to offset the price reductions? On the other hand, on average, a mere 2% price increase is profitable even if you lose 8% of your volume. But you have to *earn* the price increase from your customers.

Second, think long-term. If you do reduce prices and increase profits, will it be sustainable? Your competitors will quickly become aware of your moves and probably match your new pricing structure. People will treat you the way you train them. Don't think so? Look at the plight of the American auto companies and airlines. They have trained customers to wait for a sale, rebate, or other promotion. It's a hole they can't crawl out of.

Third, cut prices now, then try to raise them later. How do you think your customers will react? You're going to have to earn these price cuts all over again just to get even. Like General Patton said, "I don't' like to pay for the same ground twice."

Still need convincing. Segregate your customers, i.e., see what percentage of your customers account for what percent of sales. If your company is like most companies, the 80/20 rule applies. Look at the "Where Do Profits Come From?" graph. The best 20% of your customers provide 80% of your profits. Add in the middle 60% of your customers, and your at 110 to 120% of your bottom line. How? Because you lose your shirt on the worst 20% of your customers. Get rid of them.

Improving Profitability   If you are not going to cut prices to increase revenues, how do you improve your profitability? By

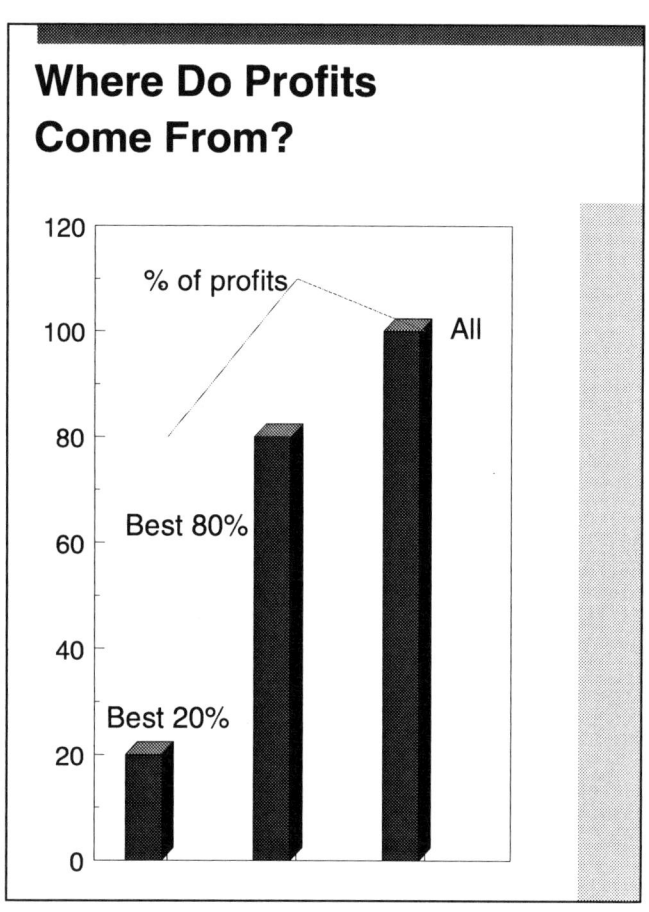

improving the profitability of your customer mix — by strengthening your position with your most profitable customers. Rather than blindly building market share, build market share from your most profitable customers. Because your competitors are likely cutting prices and sacrificing quality and service, you can easily differentiate your company by providing the services that a large portion of your customers' need — which they are willing to pay for. But, be forewarned, this approach is much more difficult and management intensive than simply cutting prices. Here's how to implement your plan:

Step 1. Figure out the real profitability of each customer. That's price, less cost of goods sold/services provided -- including discounts, credit terms, rebates, other allowances and the hardest of all — costs-to-serve. For example, do you have certain customers who demand and you provide special prices, then they also require special handling? Costs-to-serve are the "stealth" costs, out of sight relative to a specific customer. Cost-to-serve can cause customer profitability to vary as much as 50% for the same pricing terms. Attach cost-to-serve to the customers that demand them to make intelligent decisions. Why are costs-to-serve stealth? Because we don't put "tags" on our below-the-line costs (typically selling, general and administrative, SG&A) and trace them to the customer that consumes them. We normally look at SG&A as total amounts, and complain they are too high as a percent of sales, but we don't know why.

Step 2. In our time compressed environment, determine which non-price needs are most important to your profitable customers. How? Ask them. One, they will be flattered you asked. Second, they become part of the process, your partner. Simple, but it works. For example, your high-profit customers may want you to do only a simple product/service modification that they are doing, or they may want a guaranteed order fill schedule or a small increase in customer support. For profitable customers, these are far more valuable than a small price reduction trying to capture an increase in sales.

Step 3. If you undertake a program to provide these services, you will probably find yourself (1) engaging in benchmarking to determine the "gap" that exists between your performance and the best in class; (2) adopting operational performance measures so real-time information is available to respond to customers; and (3) empowering your employees with self-directed work teams so employees can become more productive.

Don't Pay Employees for Working

Towers Perrin, an international management consulting firm, studied 80 skill-based pay systems at 27 manufacturing and service companies. The programs average four years old, and many were being "fined-tuned" to fit changing needs. On the average, the programs covered 450 employees. The study quoted one person as saying "Why did we adopt skill-based pay? I can give you the answer in two words: continuous improvement." Although skill-based pay can be used to introduce new ways of doing things, most companies use it to reinforce other efforts such as self-directed work teams. One executive noted, "Skill-based pay supports the development of teamwork."

This was a good first effort by Towers Perrin. Unfortunately, the survey communicated only with management personnel responsible for their skill-based pay systems. The employees who work under such systems were not included. Hopefully, Towers Perrin will conduct a separate survey of the employees.

Key Finding: Companies adopted skill-based pay to improve performance. Specific goals were cited:
- Increase productivity
- Reduce cycle times
- Improve customer satisfaction
- Improve skills for smoother, more efficient operations
- Heighten employee's interest in and/or commitment to their performance, and reduce turnover.

Key Finding: Successful users of skill-based pay confirm that it can improve bottom-line performance either directly or indirectly. Although difficult to measure, respondents reported:

- 70% reported measurable productivity improvements, 30% said they were significant
- 71% said operating costs decreased, 29% significantly
- 88% said quality had improved
- 73% reported improved job satisfaction, 18% significantly
- 75% said turnover declined.

Respondents also felt that skill-based pay reinforced skill development and broadened decision making, resulting in the following benefits:

- Develop a cross-trained, multi-skilled, work force that can tackle more tasks providing flexibility to reorganize rapidly as circumstances dictate.
- Eliminate static job classifications, which many employees think are artificial and arbitrary, often leading to "that's not my job." To work, employers must push decision-making down allowing employees to be accountable for their decisions.
- Improve information flow since continuous learning is a requirement for and a result of skill-based pay. As employees expand their skills and come into contact with more people,

Installing a Skill-Based Pay System

	First Generation Plan	Second Generation Plan
Types of skills	Mostly technical	Expand to include administrative (e.g. scheduling; budgeting) team effectiveness (e.g. coaching; problem solving)
Number of skill levels	Between 4 and 7	Skill levels either increased (to provide more opportunities) or decreased (for greater administrative ease)
Method of assessing skill proficiency	Team leaders or supervisors	Peer review
Plan eligibility	Generally limited to production employees	Expand to include office, clerical, shipping and technical personnel; in a few cases, even management

they learn how their responsibilities (not job) fit into the whole, sparking questions, ideas and useful suggestions.

- Focus on the end product or service, the result, not the job, to force employees to find better ways to serve the customer faster, but with less effort.

Key Finding: The success of skill-based pay depends on top management investing in its employees. Seventy five percent of the companies said their pay rates were higher than market and 60% said they spent significantly more on training. But, if the program works, total labor costs decline as a percent of cost of sales. Why? Because the flexibility increases productivity, which more than compensates for the additional compensation.

If you believe that higher pay rates will hurt, rather than help, your competitiveness, you probably are not a good candidate for skill-based pay. Thus, a non-traditional, open, participative, management attitude is a necessity which must encompass:
- A high level of trust in your employees' abilities
- Strong employee involvement in developing the program
- Management appreciation of increased flexibility
- A belief that investing in employees is worthwhile.

"Employees are our most valuable asset" has to be more than a saying. (Funny how we always say that, but haven't yet figured out how to put the value of our "intellectual capital" on the balance sheet.)

The Generation Gap First generation plans, naturally enough, can function as a reliable "testing ground" for employees. Over time, as employees become comfortable with skill-based pay, they tend to make enhancements and refinements. See the table Installing a Skill-Based Pay System on page 129.

Key finding: Skill-based pay programs are generally run by line-management. To succeed, you must involve employees and line-management at the earliest stages of program development to gain their support. Most companies use task forces composed of a wide array of employees at different levels and different functional areas to design and implement the programs. Although the process is very time consuming, averaging three meetings per week over a year, the companies agreed the time was well spent.

A strong communications program can avoid some difficult design problems. Middle managers find the transition from supervisor, and holder of power, to trainer and facilitator the most difficult part of skill-based pay. With early involvement, they are less threatened since they helped design the system.

Key Finding: Skill-based pay can be used for almost any employee group in virtually any environment. The first skill-based pay systems were applied to manufacturing or processing plants. Only management employees were significantly underrepresented in the study, primarily because of the difficulty of isolating skill blocks. Forty-one percent of the companies said their programs covered all employees in the plant, department, or location. The balance selectively covered functions, but didn't limit them to production or operations. Also included were sales, customer service, and clerical employees.

But what about skill-based pay systems in a union environment? Thirty-one percent of the companies operate in a union environment and their systems appeared as successful as non-union companies. How? Solicit union involvement early to establish and maintain trust.

Consider these special design provisions to ease the transition:

Grandfathering. Provide a sufficient amount of time, perhaps two years for workers with seniority and high pay rates, to acquire the requisite skills to function under the new system.

Use union trainers. This will foster union support since it sends a message that you aren't trying to push the union out.

Greenfield sites. Although skill-based pay can work in most locations, it's easiest to implement at brand new sites. There's no existing culture or reward system to modify. All employees start with no seniority.

Key Finding: Testing skill mastery must be stringent, yet fair, and must identify employees' abilities and evaluate their

usefulness on an ongoing basis. Assessing and certifying employee skills is a crucial part of the program:
- The assessment determines initial pay rates and then how, when, and how much for pay raises.
- Regular reviews make certain that skills remain relevant; technological changes demand new skills. If employees can't pass the test, they loose the pay for that skill until they do pass. Again, periodic recertification ensures continued competence.
- Companies used several different approaches in assessing employee skills. The most common was peer review where employees demonstrate their competence to their team or work cell. Others used a committee or co-workers on other shifts to make assessments. Surprisingly, there was no evidence that employees would "help out a buddy" by certifying unacceptable performance. Peers actually held coworkers to a higher standard.
- Team leader or supervisor assessment was the second most common method using traditional one-on-one sessions. But, just as in a traditional setting, these assessments were criticized as too subjective, inconsistent, and communicated performance issues poorly.
- Third party observation handled by either an individual - such as a trainer - or an assessment center.

For skill retention, half the companies required employees to use their skills for higher pay rates. Twenty percent don't require employees to master skills they won't use. Others used job rotation to maintain skill competence. Finally, some recertified skills, thus making the employee responsible for maintaining their skills to collect the incremental pay.

Key Finding: There are no magic formulas for developing skill sets or levels. The companies included 4 to 18 skill levels, with 4 to 7 being most common, but as many outside that range were successful as inside it. Further, of the companies entering their second generation skill-based pay system, as many were increasing their skill levels as decreasing them. All were confident the change would be an improvement. Those companies increasing the number of skill levels felt they were increasing opportunities to prevent employees from "topping out." Those companies decreasing the levels were attempting to make the program easier to understand, and were reducing administrative complexity.

For the companies surveyed, skill-based pay is improving performance, employee commitment, and solving the problem of a shrinking pool of skilled labor. However, skill-based

pay isn't for every company. In order to be successful, you must address the following issues:
- The nature of the jobs and operations
- Your organizational climate
- Your employees' attitudes
- Your training resources
- Your assessment and testing procedures
- Your pay structure and salary policies.

CEOs warned

Companies must take worker empowerment issues seriously to retain their competitive edge. This was the conclusion of a study sponsored jointly by the National Association of Manufacturers (NAM) and the U.S. Department of Labor (DOL). The study was broad-based using 14 (1 per city) focus groups to interview 113 CEOs and front-line workers representing companies with fewer than 100 employees. More than 3,000 people were interviewed. In two cities, the worker participants were all union members.

The study was launched to: ". . . encourage . . . manufacturers to create a high-performance work environment by investing in the education and training of their human resources and empowering them to make decisions that will make the manufacturers more globally competitive."

The results give comfort that things aren't as bad as the media would have us believe, but we will have to work hard to achieve gains in the future. NAM President Jerry Jasinowski noted that CEOs ". . . have a strong sense of optimism and pride in the manufacturing sector. However, . . . to remain competitive, CEOs agreed they must focus on high-quality products, productivity and customer satisfaction . . . and the key is our country's workers."

Conversely, workers, especially those not highly skilled, had a much more negative view of the future and job stability. Somewhat surprisingly, workers are anxious to receive training on company time to increase job security and to foster company loyalty. Workers warned about lack of management commitment to front-line workers, feeling not only that management sees production workers as less valuable and more easily replaced, but also that management consistently ignored workers as worthwhile consultants. Workers felt they could contribute the most, but were never asked, and had no faith that they would be rewarded even if their suggestions were adopted.

Both management and workers agreed that improved communication is the key to the trust needed for a high-performance work environment. But, CEOs and workers had widely divergent views on communication. All recognized the need to re-think the processes around which work is organized; to incorporate the principles of Total Quality Management. All agreed that training is important. Pressure to change comes from competition and customers.

CEOs thought change was occurring at half the required pace. Most CEOs were learning from the successes of other companies. Cost-conscious CEOs were leery of the benefits of general education programs. In response, several have adopted successful apprenticeship programs. Even though CEOs couldn't quantify education spending, they weren't concerned that increased skills would make workers transient. In fact, most felt the "investment" would pay off. For help and guidance, CEOs turned to their peers who were willing to share information and experiences openly with non-competitors.

Both workers and CEOs agreed that to increase productivity and remain competitive, companies must:
1. Improve communication
2. Continually develop and upgrade worker skills
3. Empower front-line workers to use these skills
4. Make a total commitment to quality in all products and processes

Conclusion: The most troubling aspect of this study is that there continues to be a wide gulf between management and workers, as to how each views the other's communication effort. Management thinking it is doing a good job, but front-line workers are saying, "Not yet."

Management should reexamine how it is doing. Unfortunately, management usually can not come to a valid conclusion trying to assess its own effectiveness. No one wants to hear bad news. Workers will think the deck is stacked against them if management conducts the survey itself. It certainly is worth the few dollars it costs to have an outside consultant conduct the survey. After all, you simply waste your money, time and effort, if the results are not valid, and they won't be if your workers give you the answers they think you want to hear. Making decisions with faulty data is worse than using "gut instinct."

Financial reporting in the 21st century

In response to mounting litigation, the American Institute of CPAs formed the Special Committee on Financial Reporting to study the needs of the users of financial statements.[7] The committee released a report titled *The Information Needs of*

---

[7] Adapted from *Improving Business Reporting — A Customer Focus, Meeting the Information Needs of Users, Comprehensive Report of the Special Committee on Financial Reporting,* AICPA, 1994.

Investors and Creditors. Edmund L. Jenkins, a partner at Arthur Anderson, Chicago and the Committee's chairman, noted that "The continued relevance of external reporting is at risk. The basic problem is that the world is rapidly changing and external reporting is not changing to keep pace."

To find out what users need, the committee analyzed the writings of investors and creditors and the types of information included in analyst's formal reports. The committee met with portfolio managers and bankers (large and small) and the Financial Accounting Policies Committee of the Association for Investment Management and Research, among others. The committee found traditional audited financial statements fail to meet users' critical information needs: relevance, reliability, comparability, and neutrality.

Just like war is too important to be left to the military, financial reporting is too important to be left to accountants. The committee acknowledged that credibility of financial reporting is a serious problem, that users feel management reports information in the best possible light, and, avoids reporting poor performance (It took a study to come to that conclusion?). Further, the committee found that "(u)sers of financial information are a diverse group with diverse information needs." The current system of financial reporting is analogous to shopping for a pair of shoes, and only having one choice — what the shoe manufacturer thinks you need. Users of financial information are no longer willing to blindly accept whatever the accounting profession proffers.

The report opines that financial reporting is central to the operation of effective capital markets by providing relevant and reliable information to reduce risks and uncertainties. The result of the study is a plan to substantially and radically change the scope and nature of financial reporting. To meet the needs of users, the committee recommends the following changes in financial statements:

- Value information - Rather than replacing the current historical cost-based system, which provides consistent information, users want fair value information on certain types of long-lived assets and long-term liabilities.
- Disaggregated information - Users think the current disaggregation disclosures are inadequate to predict earnings and cash flow, on a quarterly basis. In other words, they want the same information management looks at in deciding how to run the company.
- Core earnings - Believing that management often manipulates GAAP to manage earnings through what is treated as non-recurring (i.e., non-recurring losses are given line-

item treatment while gains are treated as ordinary income), users want information about what portion of earnings is stable in order to provide a basis for estimating sustainable earnings.

* Estimates, assumptions and off-balance sheet risks - Users want more qualitative and quantitative information about risks associated with financial instruments and off-balance sheet financings. If users don't agree with the estimates and assumptions used to determine material asset and liability amounts, they can make adjustments themselves.
* Non-financial performance measures - Users want to know what the company's key success factors are and how they "drive," and are reported in, the financial statements.
* Forward-looking information - Users want information on which to base their own projections, including, near-term opportunities and risks that are relatively certain and quantifiable.
* Users want auditors to provide additional qualitative assurance in their reports.

If one takes the Jenkins' Committee's report to its logical conclusion, to satisfy varied needs of users of financial statements, the result will be auditors certifying a database of information that users can then assemble any way they want. Investment banking and commercial banking analysts already do so by tearing apart the audited statements and reassembling them. In fact, that's how Ray Dirks, research director of RAS Securities, uncovered the Equity Funding of America stock-fraud case.[8]

Quanex is a billion dollar specialty mini-steel manufacturer based in Houston. I recently gave the 25 or so controllers a private presentation, which I'll discuss more under Extraordinary Guarantees. Quanex publishes more nonfinancial performance measurement information in its annual report than any public company I've seen. During my presentation, I asked the Controller why. He said the company wants its competitors to know how good they are at meeting deadlines and customer specifications, so the competitors don't even try to compete on those issues.

Sources of industry and company information

One of the required tools to be competitive in the 1990s, and beyond, is access to information. Computerized data bases exist that contain three different types of information: filings with the SEC, research reports by investment banking firms, and general

---

[8] Big Entertainment Prospectus Offers Thrills and Chills, *The Wall Street Journal*, October 18, 1992, page C6.

business news and information. These data bases are on CD-ROM and are menu driven, so no programming skills are required — anyone can learn to use them in 15 minutes. Each of these data bases is updated quarterly.

These sources provide both the auditor and the corporate financial manager with tremendous research capabilities. Unfortunately, the systems are not cheap. If needed only occasionally, it is usually less expensive to conduct your searches through an on-line service, such as CompuServe or Dialog. Alternatively, most public libraries in major cities have one or more of these CD-ROM data bases and allow use of them at no charge. Most universities also have these databases for faculty, staff and students.

All of these systems are PC compatible, and the needed information in the database can be viewed on the screen, printed out, or downloaded to a floppy disk for printing on another personal computer. If the researcher uses any of the databases at the library, take a number of formatted floppies of the proper size and density. Since some of the systems assign the same name to every download, any additional searches will be assigned the same file name, overwriting and destroying any previous download. To prevent this problem, use a different floppy disk for each download.

SEC Filings. The full text and numerous subsections of all SEC filings for every actively traded public company for the past five years is available from three database operators: Compact Disclosure, Disclosure, Inc. and SEC Online on SilverPlatter. "Pink sheet" companies, which are less actively traded, are not included on any of these databases. Although produced by different companies, all of these databases operate in essentially the same manner.

> **... existing customers are worth five times more than new customers.**

For example, auditors can search the databases to find all public companies in the plastics industry (by using SIC code) with sales between $50 and $250 million, with at least 500 employees and a working capital ratio of at least 1.55 to 1, with less than $2 million in R & D last year, located east of the Mississippi.

With the ability to find financial statements of comparable public companies at the touch of a few buttons, auditors are in a much better position to audit beyond the books, and into the business.

Investment banking research reports. The Investext database contains several hundred thousand research reports by nearly 300 investment banking, brokerage, and research firms on actively traded public companies in the U.S. These research reports are extremely important to learn what research analysts think of a particular industry and how they analyze it using information in SEC filings and broad-based industry research. Auditors can use Investext to build their "intellectual capital" to understand the ramifications of non-financial performance measures.

Investext contains the operational performance measures that analysts use to determine the financial health of companies in a particular industry. For example, in the software industry, many analysts use revenue per employee as a productivity benchmark. Carry the analysis one step further to determine where the subject company's productivity comes from. Is it from ongoing operations such as new product sales, or from one-time licensing fees?[9] Or, if prompt, accurate delivery of the company's product or service is important to customer satisfaction, the analyst will quantify the impact of variations in delivery performance.

Or consider any company that replicates its concept in multiple locations. For a fast-food restaurant chain, analysts will determine what portion of the company's revenue change is from new units opened in the prior 12 months (called "new

---

[9] For a complete discussion, see "Measuring the RIGHT Performance for Competitive Superiority," *The Competitive Superiority Report: How "Ordinary" Companies Thrive on Competition*, July 1992, pp. 1 - 5, Gary Zeune & Associates, Columbus, Ohio.

store sales") and what portion is from changed sales at units more than 12 months old (called "old store sales"). The analysts will be concerned with the sustainability of revenue growth if the majority of growth comes from new units, and the company has fewer units scheduled to open in the current year than the prior year.

General Business Data. The ABI/INFORM business data base contains citations and abstracts of over 125,000 articles from over 800 business magazines and journals. This database is searched using key words. For example, a researcher could find over 400 articles on IPOs in less than 10 minutes, copy them to floppy disks, and print them out at the office.

Several other sources of information are available. Although not available on CD-ROM, these are extremely helpful:

- Annual Statement Studies - Robert Morris Associates - Financial and operating ratios for 300 lines of business include balance sheet composites by company size, profit and loss data.
- Almanac of Business and Industrial Financial Ratios, Leo Troy, Ph.D., Prentice-Hall.
- Key Business Ratios - Dun and Bradstreet ratios from 125 lines of manufacturing, wholesaling, retailing, and construction industries.

Why productivity programs fail

Over 50 percent of all attempts to increase productivity fail in the first four years. Why? Three major reasons exist.

First, consultants don't have to live with their recommendations. If their advise doesn't work, they suffer no consequences. Consultants have to have a new consulting "widget" to sell every year. And many give their widget a spiffy new name and a new package each year to generate more business.

The second factor I characterize as "the rhetoric is running ahead of the reality." Remember when, in the early 1980s IBM standardized the PC? "Experts" were predicting that by 1985 there would be a PC in every home and on every desk and paper would disappear. Has this happened yet? In fact, the opposite happened. Because it became so easy to make changes, people were no longer willing to live with small errors, and instead corrected what they previously would have let stand uncorrected.

The third factor is the tendency to measure efforts instead of results. A few months ago, a business reporter from the *Columbus (Ohio) Dispatch* interviewed the owner of a local private company that was instituting a quality program. The reporter asked how it was going. The owner responded, "Great. At the end of next week, over 90 percent of our employees will have gone through our quality training program." The obvious next question, which the reporter didn't ask, was, "So, what difference did it make? Is quality higher? Has customer satisfaction improved? Is your repeat business rate up?" The owner was measuring effort. That's OK, for starters. But, the real issue is, Did the training make any difference?

There are two major types of productivity program failures. First is the fizzle or fade out problem. CEOs pass the program to someone down in the organization. Productivity programs nearly always flatten the organizational structure. The result is that many middle managers lose their power base -- the right to tell lower level employees what to do and the ability to withhold information. Many times, asking a middle manager to implement the productivity program is to ask them to work themselves out of a job. The result? Middle managers will sabotage the effort.

The second reason for program failures is many are set up to fail. Consider the case of the public utility that instituted a TQM program on Tuesday, and on Thursday announced a 15 percent work force reduction. Which do you think got the employees attention?

Preventing failure

So how do you prevent failure? There's no sure fire method, because each company is different. Each company has its own unique personality. But, a few common elements come to mind.

Top management support Top management can send the right signal by managing the effort themselves. Probably the most ingenious technique of communicating the seriousness of the effort was used by Robert Galvin. Then CEO of Motorola in the mid-1980s, Galvin found that Motorola's defect rate in computer chips was 8,800 per million produced. But the major Japanese manufactures had a defect rate of only 3.4 parts per million.

To get everyone's' attention, Galvin sent an e-mail to all 200,000 Motorola employees, "Our quality stinks! Bob Galvin." From that point on, every one who had a meeting with Galvin had to begin by explaining what they were doing in their area to improve quality. Ingenuous, very simple, and cost free.

Empower your employees You might say you give your employees the authority to take of care your customers. First, stop saying "My customers." Say, "Our customers." Customers belong to every employee they come in contact with. You probably hold your employees *responsible* for taking care of customers, but give them the *authority* to take care of them.

Ritz-Carlton Hotels won the Malcolm Baldrige National Quality Award for service. How? One of the major reasons is giving all employees, even housekeepers, the authority to spend up to $2000 to satisfy any customer complaint. Do you trust your front-line employees that much? Think

> **If you were arrested for customer service, would there be enough evidence to convict you?**

how much more time you would have to work on strategic issues if you gave front-line employees the authority to resolve 95 percent of all customer issues.

Ever heard of Federal Express? Did you know that FedEx gives its truck drivers authority to spend up to $250 to take care of any customer problem? Does an employee ever make a mistake? Of course they do. They aren't like management — which never makes a mistake.

Measure and reward the desired performance   An auto manufacturer was having a terrible time with defective engine blocks. Very expensive to manufacture, the defect rate was excessive. The solution? Send every plant employee through TQM training. After spending nearly $1 million over three years, the defect rate decreased only slightly. The company called in a consultant who looked over the situation and said, " For $50,000, I'll tell you what's wrong. And if it doesn't work, you don't have to pay me." Eager to solve the problem, the company readily agreed. The consultant told the company to change two words on one form.

The plant manager was paid a base salary and a bonus tied to the number of blocks his operation shipped to the assembly plant. The consultant correctly identified the major problem. The plant manager was being paid for quantity, not quality. His pay was changed to base salary and a bonus tied to *net good* blocks shipped. Once the company stopped paying for defective production, it solved the whole problem.

Another example. KPMG Peat Marwick studied what it considered successful clients. The major finding was that the most successful companies pushed the decision making down to the lowest level with the skills to take care of the customer.

These companies had three characteristics in common:
1. Management listened to their customers. What did the customers want? What was right/wrong with current products/services?
2. Management analyzed whether the company could fill the gaps between customer wants and company capabilities.

3. The companies involved their employees to close the gaps between what customers wanted and what the company was providing.

Change isn't easy

After the initial enthusiasm, reality will set in when employees begin to find out how hard change is. You start your productivity program thinking things will only improve. This almost never happens. In short order, productivity will begin to decline, for a few weeks to several months (see "The Change Process" diagram). Why? While employees are figuring out new ways to do things, they forget to serve their customers. Employees may get so engrossed in improving the work processes, they might forget to return customer calls.

Many companies that give up on productivity programs or don't have the staying power, quit at the bottom of the curve. Of course, what signal do you send to employees? The next time you want to try a new management technique, the reaction is, "Just wait a month or two, it'll go away." Just like diseases are now resistant to drugs, you have inadvertently made your employees more resistant to future productivity changes.

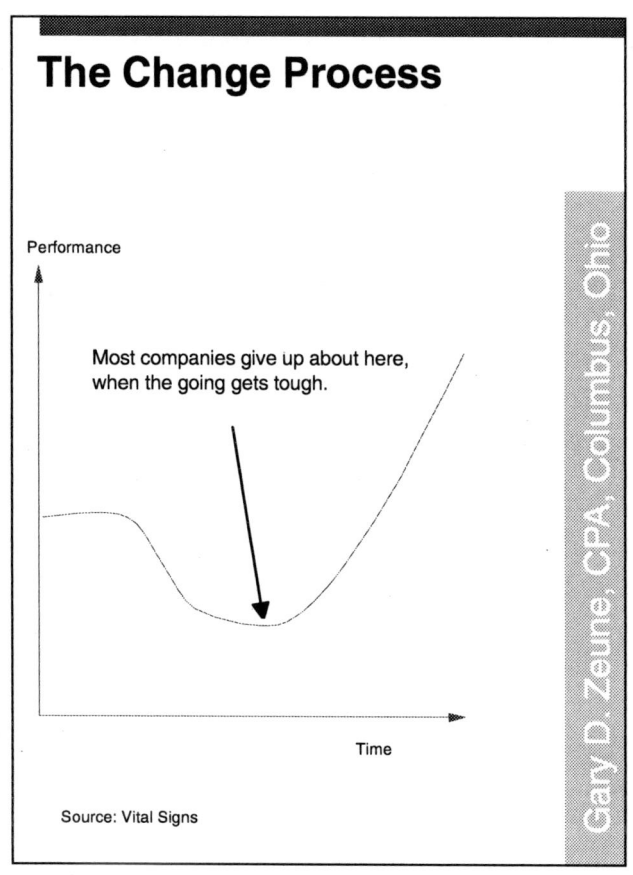

What kind of company do you work at?

Here's a quick, easy test to tell whether your company operates on a world-class basis. Below are three pairs of words. Circle one word in each pair.

What Kind of Company Do Your Work At?			
Question	Answer 1		Answer 2
Does your company run by:	Rules?	or	Results?
Does your company favor	Individuals?	or	Teams?
Is you company satisfied with the	Status quo?	or is it a	Risk taking company?

If all your answers are in the Answer 2 column, you're in good shape. If you had just one circle in the Answer 1 column, you've got changes to make. After all, if a company is satisfied with the status quo, it's standing still. Think about this. If your company is still doing the same thing this year as it did last year, if it's standing still in serving its customers, it's going backwards. How can this be true? Think of yourself as a customer for any product or service. Do you make a decision in a vacuum? No. You judge what's available to you *relative to what else is available in the market*. So do your customers judge your company — in comparison to your competitors. If you are not making progress, but your competitors are, your customers perceive that your company is going backwards in serving their needs, and you are at a competitive disadvantage.

Extraordinary guarantees

One technique to light a fire in your organization is to provide an extraordinary guarantee. Extraordinary Guarantees are above and beyond the industry standard. First, Extraordinary Guarantees "signal" customers (that's a fancy word for sending customers a "message") that you stand above the crowd. Second, Extraordinary Guarantees also signal employees that you believe they can satisfy customer demands. Extraordinary Guarantees almost always result in reduced operating costs, because the threat of pay outs to compensate customers for failure focuses employees' attention on streaming lining operations, and internal cooperation.

Extraordinary Guarantees send a powerful message to customers. Automatic Data Processing in Roseland, NJ, monitors the frequency of phone calls from clients to forewarn ADP of problems in the making. American Business Information in Omaha, Nebr.. provides a money-back guarantee on its CD-ROM products. So far, only about 200 of 450,000 annual customers have asked for their money back. To combat a poor service image, cable TV companies are giving customers $20 refunds if service calls or installations aren't made on time. Indiana University in Bloomington offers "gradpact," assuring students with passing grades that they will get a degree in four years.

I try to put my money where my mouth is and follow my own advice. In late 1994, I got a call from the Controller of Quanex, a $1 billion public company based in Houston. Each year the company holds a three day meeting, bringing in all division controllers from around the world, about 25 or so. The Controller had read one of my articles on benchmarking in *The Financial Managers' Report* (AICPA), and asked me to give a private presentation. When he asked how much it would be for a half-day class, he about fell off his chair, saying that even though I would be the first outside speaker, the $3,000 price seemed awfully expensive. I told him that I don't carry receivables, I expect to be paid at the conclusion of the presentation. I further told him I guarantee my presentations, and pay my own travel expenses. So how does all this work? The class would be a flat fee, including travel. He was to bring a check with him to the class. If at the end of the class anyone was not happy and didn't think they got at least twice the cost of the class in benefit, he didn't have to give me the check. No questions asked. Following is my standard guarantee included in all my course brochures.

> **100% NO-RISK GUARANTEE**
>
> *Mr. Zeune's courses are consistently rated at least 4.7 on a 5.0 scale. If you are not satisfied for any reason, there are no fees or expenses.*

Why do I give this guarantee? Because I want any work I do to be risk-free to my clients. My accounting friends, billing by the hour for their effort, can't believe I give this guarantee. "Too risky," they say. My response? "How many clients do you think have refused to pay me? (None) After all, if a client isn't happy with my work when it's done and won't pay me, then what's the likelihood they will pay me in 30 days if I send them a bill? And if they aren't happy with my work, why should they pay me?"

Another example of an extraordinary guarantee is Selectron. Based in Eden Prairie, Minnesota, Selectron repairs computer mother boards. Management at Selectron knows that if they repair a mother board, and it malfunctions a short time later, the customer will assume Selectron damaged it while fixing the original problem. Selectron's solution? The company has enough experience that employees repair not only the original problem, but parts likely to fail, and then guarantee the *entire board* for two years.

Selectron doesn't charge it's customers for the additional repairs. Selectron found it was cheaper to repair items likely to fail, while they had the board, than to deal with an angry customer, and still lose the customer's future business. How much business do you think Selectron has?

A couple of years ago, a consulting client introduced me to another business owner, a local roofing contractor. The economy was slowing down. The contractor didn't want to lay off employees, but didn't have the money to do any kind of advertising or marketing. Of course, the home improvement business doesn't have a very good reputation, and the barriers to entry are low. Anyone with a tool belt and a hammer can hold themselves out as a contractor. Word of mouth, through satisfied customers, is the most effective advertising tool for a small contractor.

But how do you spread the gospel? I asked my client if he guaranteed his work. "Yes, for a year," he said. "Have you ever called a customer near the end of the warranty period to find out if they need any repairs done?", I asked. "No," he said. So, he set about calling customers whose guarantees were about to expire. The result? For every dollar he spent on repairs of items he probably would not other have otherwise had to spend under the guarantee, he earned $11 in additional revenues from word-of-mouth advertising, plus more through referrals. When was the last time you called a customer asking whether you can repair something under warranty? It's a competitive advantage. Your competitors will think one of two things: Either you must be suicidal, or your work must be perfect (and they can't compete). Neither is true.

What prevents an Extraordinary Guarantee? Principally three things. First, if you don't have the ability to track and identify customer needs and wants. Second, if you can't generate enough enthusiasm in your employees. Third, if your organization structure is cumbersome and prevents front-line employees from taking care of customer problems.

What is required to implement an Extraordinary Guarantee? Four things. First, hold an executive round-table discussion to answer this question, "Why do customers do business with us?" Then hold focus group sessions to get some preliminary ideas of what your customers think. Next, prepare a preliminary survey instrument. Finally, do a large scale survey.

Second, most companies find they have to streamline operations. If you make it cumbersome for customers to trigger your guarantee, you've defeated the value of the guarantee, and taught customers they can't trust you.

Third, push decision-making down. This usually means you need to give front-line workers the training they need to take care of customers. Think of how much time executives will have to work on really important issues if they don't have to take care of minor customer problems. And, think how much happier your customers will be if their problems are solved while they are on the phone, rather than having to wait for a call-back, after the customer service representative gets an OK to solve the problem. Enthusiastic customers are much more profitable.

Fourth, the first three changes are for naught if you don't improve the original service.

When are Extraordinary Guarantees a good idea? If your company has achieved a high level of quality and the market hasn't recognized it yet. Also, when your employees are ready to implement an Extraordinary Guarantee.

When Extraordinary Guarantees are not a good idea First, avoid Extraordinary Guarantees if you aren't prepared to produce quality that you are willing to stand behind, or if your quality can't be recognized quickly enough to offset the costs of achieving it.

Second, if there are significant factors outside your control, an Extraordinary Guarantee does not make sense. For example, an airline would be foolish to offer an unconditional on-time arrival guarantee. Few airlines can control the weather. But, airlines should offer a no mechanical breakdown guarantee. Such a guarantee would "signal" flyers that the airline maintains its planes in top condition. Finally, if the company has a few large customers, any one of which could trigger the guarantee and do you serious harm, avoid an Extraordinary Guarantee.

Another example of an Extraordinary Guarantee is Ford Motor Company's introduction of the 1996 Taurus. Ford offered a special 24-month lease in certain regions of the country to owners of Camry and Accord sedans. The lease let Taurus owners escape their lease after six months with no penalty. "It really shows that Ford has a great deal of confidence in this car," commented Christopher Cedergren, an auto-industry analyst with AutoPacific Group in Santa Ana, Calif.[10]

---

[10] The Engine Driving the Taurus: It's Marketing, *The Wall Street Journal,* September 11, 1995, p. B1.

Competing based on service

"Unhappy news travels fast: It's no secret that good service pays off. But a study done for a division of American Airlines, parent AMR, quantifies the cost of poor customer service. The survey found that one unhappy passenger tells nine to 13 other people about his or her bad experience. One happy flier tells just five people. Just 4% of unhappy customers complain, but for every person who complains, there are 24 unhappy customers who don't say anything. Of those who complain, 82% to 95% will do business with the company again if their problem gets solved quickly. But 75% to 90% of those 24 unhappy and uncomplaining customers will never do business with the company again, the study says."[11] You can't spend enough marketing dollars to overcome that kind of word of mouth damage. The complainers are the "1s" in the Xerox study.

If it costs 5 times more to get a new customer than to keep an existing customer, can you afford not to make a dissatisfied customer happy? And do it quick. Authorize front-line employees to take care of the customer.

But, manufacturers are constantly told to strive for zero defects. Because it takes the same resources to get from 95 to 100 percent (i.e., zero defects) in quality as from zero to 95 percent quality, companies are focusing on competing in a

---
[11] *USA Today*, May 21, 1996.

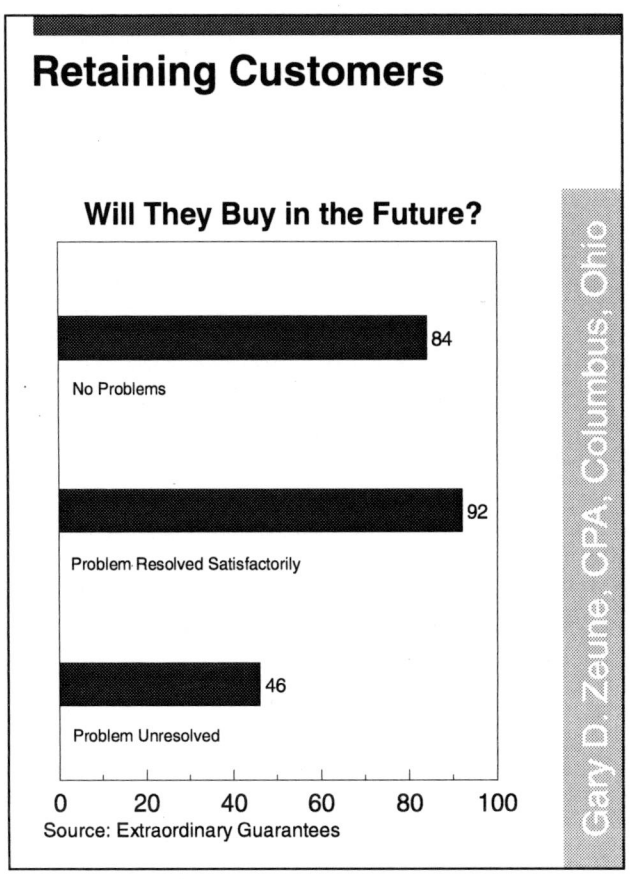

different manner. Several surveys (see "Retaining Customers" graph) have found that customers are more likely to buy again from a company with which they have had a problem satisfactorily resolved, than they are to buy again from a company with which they have never had a problem.

This seems odd. Why would a customer be more likely to buy from a company with which he or she had a problem? Answer: Because the customer has tested the company's promise to fix, repair, replace, whatever, and it works. The customer now has a frame of reference, a sense of comfort, and is satisfied. On the other hand, if the customer has never experienced a problem, the customer does not know how the company will respond if a problem is encountered.

What do you do with this strategic information? Companies have decided it's cheaper to put their resources into satisfactorily solving a few customer problems, rather than striving for zero defects.

Customer loyalty can increase profits 26 to 85 percent,[12] and is the key to long-term profitability. Several studies have shown that satisfying customer's needs is more than important to most employees than a pay raise. Self-directed work teams are one way to implement this strategy. More on this later.

A property and casualty insurance company found that customer satisfaction dropped from 75 percent to 55 percent when the customer service representative left, and customer

---

[12] "Putting the Service-profit Chain to Work," *Harvard Business Review*, March 1994.

retention fell. Thus, management began measuring each rep's customer turnover, and took steps to reduce rep turnover by thinking of training as an investment, not an expense.

Define your loyal customers; who become more profitable over time. Measure "depth-of-relationship." Depth-of-relationship measures how many of your products or services a customer buys. It's much more profitable to sell one more product or service to an existing customer than to incur the cost of enticing a new customer into buying.

Referrals are another profitable niche. Provide your loyal customers with discount coupons they can give to referrals.

Customer defections are very costly. Do you track where defectors go, and why they defected to a competitor? Conduct exit interviews. A credit card company found that when it conducted exit interviews, showing customers it cared, even when leaving, the company retained 1/3 of the defectors.

Self-directed work teams

Many world-class companies have discovered the power of self-directed work teams. Self-directed work teams are characterized by small groups of employees responsible for an entire work process. This structure breaks down barriers caused by the traditional functional organization. However, you can't simply tell people to work in a different relationship with their peers. If it's to work, employees must be trained in communications to solve team problems, together.

Remember, it's the result we're interested in, not how the work gets done. Thus, self-directed work teams won't solve problems the way management would solve them. Teams must be allowed to make mistakes. Management must trust that the team members will make decisions right for the company. This assumes, of course, that all of the company's systems are goal-congruent.

Self-directed work teams are not quality circles. Popularized in Japan, quality circles don't make decisions; quality circles make only recommendations.

There are four requirements for successful self-directed work teams. First, the team must have a clear sense of identity. The team must have objectives that can be measured. Second, the team's objectives must support the corporation's mission statement. Third, the team must be held accountable to meet the objectives. Fourth, the team must comply with fiscal, legal and other company guidelines.

The transfer of decision-making authority takes place gradually, over a period of several years. As illustrated in the Self-directed Work Teams graph on page 174, there are five

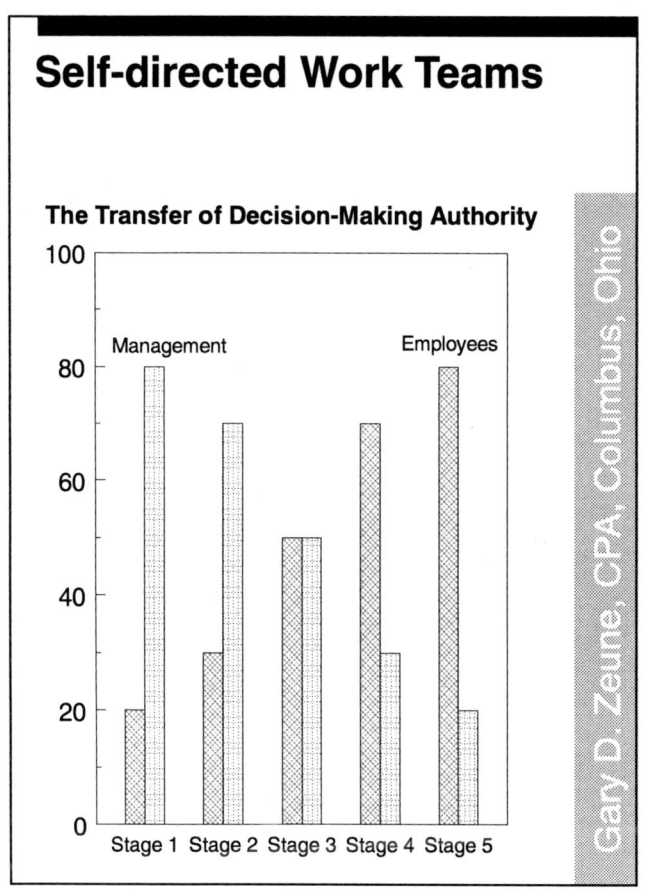

stages to transfer decision-making authority: start-up, state-of-confusion, leader-centered teams, tightly-formed teams, self-directed teams.

Stage 1: Start-up Recognize that you cannot legislate productivity. Employees must want to perform at a peak level. Let the team do its own thing, but establish boundaries of behavior so the team will know what it is expected to work on. The team members must be given "awareness training" to prepare them for the impact their success will have on the company. Middle managers will be especially threatened since self-directed work teams will take over many of their responsibilities.

Middle managers have two bases of power. The ability to tell subordinates what to do, and the ability to withhold information from subordinates. Self-directed work teams absorb these basis of power. Having lost their traditional power base, some middle managers will feel as though they've lost their jobs and will leave the company. The managers who stay will become "consultants" to the teams and more valuable to the company.

Select the initial team members carefully. If possible, use volunteers. Ask these questions:
- Do potential members want to expand beyond traditional roles?
- Who listens?
- Who has initiative?
- Who shares ideas?

Once the team members are selected, they master technical, administrative and interpersonal skills. Managers must set the performance expectations and adopt a formal hands-off policy. Teams must learn record keeping, reporting skills, EEO compliance and other human resource requirements.

Stage 2: State of Confusion Instead of ordering subordinates how to do the work, managers in a team environment monitor the team against clear performance standards. Successful managers will give the team new responsibilities as soon as the team is ready and act as the intermediary between the team and the company. As an intermediary, the manager will provide the team with the resources it needs to accomplish its goals.

The manager also has other responsibilities. First, the manager will clarify the team's roles and responsibilities by setting the priorities for the team to achieve its goals. Second, the manger will coordinate the various teams and support groups. As managers give up their traditional role of boss and adopt the mantle of "teacher," they will begin to focus on results, rather than job functions. Successful managers will transfer their skills to team members and take pride in "team" successes.

Stage 3: Leader-Centered Teams At this juncture, the team is not ready to rotate jobs in the true self-directed sense. The team still needs a strong leader, but the leader should be someone on

the team. Look for a leader that will infuse the team with an identity, using the following guidelines:
- Strong interpersonal and relationship skills
- Knows most team members' jobs
- Strong commitment to the team

Stage 4: Tightly-Formed Teams Now it's time to start building a two-way information flow and sharing. Gone will be protectionism, exclusivity and rigid demands on "how" the work gets done. The focus will be more on results. Management can begin to hand off more responsibilities according to the plan.

Stage 5: Self-directed Teams As the team gains experience in making its own decisions, the team members will begin to rotate their positions. Everyone gets a chance to play "boss" for a defined period of time. At Toledo Scale's Worthington, Ohio plant, selected as one of the 12 best manufacturing plants in the U.S. several years ago, the team members rotate jobs every 5 weeks.

A fully functional team will be:
- Flexible, conforming to changing conditions, with little required input from management, but with significant input from customers.
- Fluid, available for different uses.
- Lean, teams don't have much extra capacity.

- Responsive, able to react quickly to new challenges.
- Proactive, with the foresight to prevent problems, before customers call complaining.

Self-directed work teams are the hardest on mid-level mangers, who often have to give up their power base of giving orders and withholding information. Mid-managers must become teachers and coaches. Many won't be able to make the trip. Here are some Advantages and Disadvantages of teams:

Self-directed Work Teams	
Advantages	Disadvantages
Continuously improving quality	Doesn't always fit with company culture
Increased productivity	Significant training required
Improved customer satisfaction	Unmet goals
Significant startup overhead	Resistance from those afraid of change
Much quicker decisions	Resentment at forced change
Improved morale	Unions can scuttle the effort
Greater employee commitment	
Increased profitability	

Do Innovative Workplace Practices Pay Off?

YES! Motorola estimates that it earns $30 for every dollar it invests in employee training. Edy's Grand Ice Cream says its new employee management system reduced inventory 66%, improved productivity 57%, and increased unit sales volume

830%. Xerox, working with its unions, reduced manufacturing costs 30% and cut new product development time in half. A 1993 study of 700 companies in all major industries found those using "best practice" management techniques had a rate of return more than double companies not using such techniques.[13]

Yet many companies realize little, if any, benefit from leading edge practices. Of 100 British companies studied by A.T. Kearney, 80% gained no significant change in performance from their TQM programs. Almost two-thirds of 500 companies surveyed by Arthur D. Little had "zero competitive gain." Consultants Rath & Strong asked companies to self-grade their TQM efforts. Most gave themselves Ds and Fs.

Companies that are successful at these practices gain a competitive advantage, but it is not sustainable. As more companies adopt such practices, they lose their advantage, and result in a "running down" of the advantage to a "competitive equilibrium." Late adopters can only hope to maintain *competitive parity*. The benefit is avoiding losses that would otherwise occur from not adopting any such practices. Customers don't judge your quality, responsiveness, etc. in a vacuum. Such product or service attributes are judged in comparison to your competitors.

---

[13] *Human Resources Management Practices and Firm Performance,* Mark Huselid, working paper, IMLR, Rutgers University, June 15, 1993.

There are two approaches to improving quality. Quality products or services can be achieved by adding more inspectors and decreasing tolerances for defects after the product has been produced to the service provided. This approach rarely results in increased profits -- the increased costs usually more than consume the increased revenues. These are sometimes termed "static" returns. The cost of the improvement is merely shifted from lost orders, due to poor quality, to higher production costs.

The second approach requires fundamentally changing the way the work is done. Companies that have successfully re-engineered their processes avoid merely shifting the cost. Such gains are called "dynamic" returns. Dynamic returns are maximized by instituting mutually supporting practices; by "bundling" an integrated set of efforts. For example, implementing a JIT (just-in-time) inventory system usually involves not only reducing inventory, but the systems that support it -- Kanban card systems, lot size reduction, production "pull" systems, substantial employee training, pay for performance, and continuous change. The lowering of inventory levels makes quality problems more visible, but there's no inventory to buffer defects. Lower inventory levels force solutions if customers are to be served.

The authors found a significant relationship between JIT, and inventory turnover rates, and a firm's self-rating of quality. However, increased turnover rates did not improve plant financial performance. Further, the JIT practices were mutually supportive, i.e., the practices were more effective when implemented together.

Another group attempted to explain the lower overhead enjoyed by Japanese firms by use of JIT and lower inventory levels. They found that JIT and related techniques resulted in lower overhead only when management instituted human resource policies that involved workers in the production processes. In other words, simply lowering inventories does not, by itself, result in financial benefits. Management must promote active problem solving.

To encourage involvement, management should consider sharing the improved financial results with employees. One study noted profitability gains of 4.4%, while a second found gains of 8.4%. Many companies have instituted Employee Stock Ownership Plans (ESOP) to share the wealth, making it the most popular gain-sharing mechanism. But do ESOPs work? In public companies, if the plan is put in place to support traditional employee rewards, the stock market reacts positively. If instituted as a take-over defense mechanism, the reaction is negative.

Employees now control about 6 percent of all the equity in U.S. corporations, up from 1 to 2 percent only 10 years ago. — $525 Billion in employee-owned equity. ESOPs cover nearly 10 million employees at 9500 companies.

There are many tax advantages to ESOPs, but the most compelling reason to institute one is productivity. A 1986 study by the National Center for Employee Ownership found that sales and employment grow 8 to 11 percent faster in companies which combine employee ownership and participative management. A GAO study found that ESOP firms with open, inclusive management styles experienced annual productivity gains 52 percent higher than had they not become employee owned.[14]

However, a financial stake in the company doesn't equate to success. Success comes only if the company culture undergoes a fundamental change. If employees are going to be owners, then they must act like owners; and be willing to participate in solving problems, and share in the good times, as well as the bad.

Many ESOP companies adopt an "open-book management" style. Open-book management means that every

---

[14] "The Ins and Outs of Employee Ownership," William Landay, *Enterprise Reengineering*, July 1996, p. 1.

employee is taught to read financial statements and show how his or her job affects the financial well-being of the company. Each employee must be able to quantify his or her work. The employee should be involved in developing the measures, so the employee "owns" the measures.

There are some negatives to open-book management. One negative is the time it takes. Another is the risk to owners/managers. The amount of time it takes to open the books to employees includes:

1. The time it takes to educate employees, many of which have little, if any, understanding of financial statements. If employees don't understand the information, some of which can be complex, it could be to the company's detriment.
2. The time it takes to disseminate the information to employees and the time it takes them to digest it.
3. The time it takes to collect and incorporate employee feedback.

The risk to owners/managers is the same as any time information is shared. Employees may think they are the final evaluators of owner/manager performance, including compensation levels. If workers see the company making healthy profits, they might think they deserve a pay raise, and they might not understand why they didn't get it, but yet owners are getting large pay packages and/or investors are getting dividends. Another risk is that employees may decide to go into business for themselves, competing with the former employer. If you are thinking of open-book management, consult your attorney whether or not employees should sign a "Confidential and Non-disclosure Agreement."

Quality Products on Time

Founded in 1987, General Stair Company (GSC) had grown to $2.7 million in sales by the spring of 1994. Margins were thin, competition was intensifying, and a price war was a real possibility in the market for prefabricated stairs and railings for new residential homes. Based in Opa-Locka, Florida, business had been good, propped up by a booming south Florida home building market prompted by Hurricane Andrew, but the free ride was coming to an end.

Saby Behar, one of the co-founders, knew something radical was needed, but what? Behar wanted to offer an on-time guarantee. If the company didn't deliver on time, customers would get their money back. Timely delivery was critical to builders, which often worked on 30 or more homes simultaneously. Builders need stairs for the framing inspection, and to carry items to the second floor. Behar was determined to "brand" a commodity building product, just as Domino's had done with pizza.

Giving an extraordinary guarantee, one that's above and beyond the industry standard, is like increasing the pressure in a water hose. You will see leaks you've never seen before. Behar decided on an extraordinary guarantee. Pay customers $50 for every day the stairs were late; that being the average cost per day in additional interest builders had to pay on their construction loans.

Behar's adoption of his extraordinary guarantee forced a top to bottom reconfiguration of GSC. But first, GSC had to define what being "on-time" meant. A builder might call needing stairs for lot 56 on Tuesday, then call Wednesday saying he meant lot 36 would be ready Thursday. On Thursday, the GSC installers discovered only a hole the ground at lot 36; the builder had meant lot 46. If Behar couldn't rely on the builders' information, why not develop his own?

If GSC's employees were going to generate their own status information, they couldn't blame late deliveries on the builders any more. Accepting this challenge required a transformation in the way GSC's employees communicated and worked together. Field reps would regularly check on the status of jobs and communicate the timing of delivery and installation to the factory. Behar bought two-way radios, cellular phones, and two fax machines to fax back the schedules to the builders and build an audit trail.

Behar decided to introduce the program like a political campaign, in a hotel ballroom with balloons, buttons and T-shirts. But, a consultant told Behar it wouldn't work because his employees weren't involved in structuring the extraordinary guarantee. They had no ownership, so they wouldn't be committed to fulfilling "his" guarantee. Behar hadn't bothered to learn from his employees why the guarantee would or wouldn't work.

In early June 1994, four groups of employees began to focus on what it would take to make the guarantee work. For example, the existing two-way radio didn't have enough range to cover homes in the far north. Trucks kept breaking down. Lumber ordering didn't match production needs. Production had to handle complaints from irate customers caused by engineering not providing them with late plans. And, engineering often couldn't begin its work on time because field reps worked at their own pace. Clearly, the guarantee could be offered to builders only if every department understood how all the departments at GSC relied on each other, and provided an internal guarantee to each other.

How to motivate employees became the central question. How about free pizza? Free trips? Health insurance and a credit union, or a retirement plan? What about more money? To reduce the risk of builders making a claim under the on-time guarantee, Behar computed that, if the on-time deliveries remained at the current 95%, the company would have to put away, in a sort of self-insurance plan, $2.30 for every stair and railing installed. In an interesting twist, GSC decided to give away half of the fund balance remaining each month, after the $50 charges were paid, to five lottery winners. The other half would be paid to all employees at year end. Employees had to meet several conditions to get a share at year end: they couldn't be late more than two days a month or absent more than two days each quarter; they couldn't cause a delay, even due to an accident. Behar knew it was working when a worker accosted him after being eliminated from the first lottery. Workers cared about being included. Behar promptly handed out written rules, just to be safe.

The company also made the uncomfortable switch from salary to piece work. Labor costs were too high due to overtime needed to compensate for all the inefficiencies in the system. After the first paycheck, employees were used to it. A typical employee earning $240 in salary was earning $400 under the piece work system.

Employees became the source of numerous solutions to avoid payouts under the guarantee. One field rep developed a 12-step diagnostic tool to determine how close a house was to needing stairs installed. Another figured out how to clean dust out of sandpaper to extend its use, reducing costs. A group of employees figured out how to track loose items like screws and buttons cutting raw materials costs 5%. Everyone now saw how his or her function fit as part of the whole.

To make the guarantee real, and gain everyone's commitment, every employee signed copies: one would be given to customers, a second to formalize each department's commitment to all others, and a third in which Behar pledged to provide the necessary financial resources to carry out the program. A bonus board was hung to keep track of the bonus pool so every employee would know exactly how much was a stake at all times.

Nine months after beginning the guarantee, GSC has issued only five $50 vouchers to customers due to late deliveries. But, to maximize the bonus pool, employees might only be giving out vouchers when a customer asks for one. Ideally, they should proffer the vouchers to cement customer goodwill. But, the guarantee worked. Behar estimates the company is three times more productive now, and absenteeism is down 20%. Even though housing starts are down 5% in its market territory, GSC's business is up 20%, and margins are holding steady, even in the face of increasing competition.

Superplumber

Tom Warner was determined to revitalize his once profitable heating and air conditioning company in Washington, DC. Revenues had declined and margins went negative from 1988 to 1991. Warner decided that rather than continuing to run the company all by himself, he would enlist some of his 260 HVAC technicians to run their own micro-businesses with any and all support they needed.

FYE	'88	'89	'90	'91	'92	'93	'94
Sales	19.8	15.8	15.5	14.6	16.3	15.6	20.3
Margin	0%	-4%	-3.9%	1.4%	4.3%	3.5%	8.3%
Percentage residential	15	30	35	35	40	50	60
Percentage commercial	85	70	65	65	60	50	40
Source: *INC. Magazine*, August 1994, p. 64							

Since its founding in 1940, Warner had become the largest plumbing contractor and second-largest HVAC contractor in the DC area, riding the booming construction market for high-rise office and apartment buildings. By 1988, nearly 85% of its work was commercial. Just as Warner gained 100% ownership of the company in 1989, the overheated construction market started to cool. As property managers hired in-house plumbers, Warner was left with highly skilled techs, but no one was calling for work. Warner decided to shift his focus to residential work, but had to create a niche to compete against the hundreds of mom-and-pop operations listed in the Yellow Pages. Since Warner's image was commercial, few homeowners considered the company for residential work.

Most HVAC techs want to be in business for themselves but lack the business skills to make the break from their employers. In status conscience DC, there's a stigma associated with being a blue-collar worker, working with your hands. Running their own "business" boosts their self-esteem. One tech, Ron Inscoe, earned a maximum of $60,000 before joining Warner. In 1993, he earned $103,000 and $126,000 in 1994. Of 260 employees, by the end of 1993, 80 had become "area technical directors" (ATD).

Warner gets extraordinary effort from his techs with a generous incentive system and an organizational structure to make sure his employees earn a lot of money. Rather than making calls all over the company's market, each ATD is assigned two ZIP codes, with about 10,000 homes as an exclusive territory. This allows ATDs to develop a personal relationship with customers in their ZIP code areas.

To make certain this works, Warner had to induce his mechanics to be his sales force to promote the sale of furnaces, heat pumps, water purifiers, and service contracts. But Warner's techs weren't any different than others in the industry; they said they were plumbers, not salespeople, and didn't want to participate. Warner hired a consultant who conducted seven two-hour sessions for the 18 branch managers focusing on effective hiring, accounting, and a diverse work force. The branch managers were typically long-term employees, and good techs, but even with no formal business training, they were managing 10 to 20 people. To focus employee attention on the task at hand, Warner posted a chart in each branch showing the mix of residential/commercial work.

Residential customers wanted consistency from Warner, so Warner developed "the Warner way" of doing things, to "McDonaldsize" his business. Starting with a dozen volunteer mechanics, a consultant showed them how important they were to the sales process, and how to build their own businesses in the process. Warner wanted the ATDs to earn more than they could any place else, so they would have no desire to leave, and take customers to start their own businesses. But, it was a tall order.

ATDs would be responsible for generating their own referrals, scheduling their own work, computing their own job estimates, developing their own advertising campaigns, and collecting their own receivables. The company would support ATDs with training, trucks, phones, pagers, dispatchers, an all-night answering service, payroll and tax processing. For its part, the company committed to a $1.2 million advertising annual program. Initially featuring Warner in his Superplumber costume, the ads eventually featured ATDs in their own commercials.

To incent mechanics to be more efficient in using their time, Warner switched from time-based charges for repairs to job quoting, a flat-rate system for charging customers. The company set the charges by computing the average time to complete each type of repair. Mechanics who worked faster than the average would earn extra income. For example, mechanics are allotted 2.5 hours to change a motor. If they can do it in an hour, they still get paid for the allotted time. Mechanics also get paid for 30 minutes of travel time between appointments, even if the next job is three blocks away. This allows mechanics to spend extra time with customers and still be efficient. On average, mechanics earn about 30% of their income in bonus time.

Under the old system, mechanics had no reason to be more productive. They earned $20 an hour regardless of how long the job took. With mechanics focusing on generating more sales, the average repair ticket increased substantially; from less than $200 to nearly $400.

Fourteen of the original 18 branch managers made the trip, but only 4 of the 12 ATDs stayed with the program. Rather than fire them, Warner kept them on. He always needed top flight commercial mechanics.

To jump start each new territory, Warner mailed promo brochures to the 10,000 homes in each ATD's two ZIP codes, with a color photo of the ATD, describing his experience, and gave the company's hot line number, 800-HOT-WATER. To build business quickly, the brochures included a 10% off coupon for a $100 Homeguard service contract, which required a mechanic to be in the customer's home twice each year. And, it's the same mechanic each time, which develops personal relationships.

Mechanics even get into the act of building business. After completing a service call, mechanics leave "door hangers" for neighbors featuring a $10 off coupons saying, "Your Warner neighborhood representative has been helping a neighbor. May we help you?" The door hangers are supplemented with ads in local publications such as church bulletins and condo association newsletters. The company's business is so good and its reputation so widespread that Warner hires only one of every 25 job applicants.

In order to gain market share, Warner's 18 branches began staying open until 8 PM and Saturdays, and still charge customers regular rates, not overtime. By October 1994, evening and on Saturday work represented nearly 50% of residential work.

For the first time in his life, Tom Warner doesn't have to worry about making the phones ring.

Service with a smile

As mentioned earlier, the Ritz-Carlton Hotel chain recently won the Malcolm Baldrige National Quality Award. In her Editor's Note column in the January 1995 issue of the American Management Association's *Management Review*, Group Editor Martha Peak provides insight on how Ritz-Carlton won the award. Intrigued that employees respond, "It's my pleasure," Peak cornered Mike, the waiter, to find out why. Mike told her that "You're welcome," was perfectly acceptable, but "It's my pleasure" prevented off-hand remarks such as "no problem" or "sure thing." Mike went on that the response wasn't a put on. It really was his pleasure, and all the staff were trained to give the reply. He explained that Ritz-Carlton was the best place he had ever worked, and if he could make people happy, they would return to the hotel and he would keep his job for a long time.

But the tellers at Peak's bank were a different story. The bank advertises its tellers will greet customers as they step to the counter, or they owe the customer five dollars. But the greeting is always in a monotone, bored, with eyes glazed over. Peak concluded that both companies trained their employees to greet customers, but the bank's employees saw no connection between greetings and pay raises, promotions or continued employment. Why? Because the bank took the negative approach by deducting five dollars, as punishment, from the teller's pay if they failed to greet customers. Rewards are a much better tool to align employee interests with those of the company.

Southwest Airlines

Profiled on the cover of Fortune magazine, the question was asked, "Is Herb Kelleher [CEO of Southwest] America's best CEO?" Kelleher rejects following any particular management guru. For example, Kelleher's reaction to consultants who want to show Southwest people how to do their jobs better is "If you can do that, then I'm firing all of *them* and hiring *you*! Because [then] we've got the wrong people in those jobs. They need to solve their own problems."[15]

Such philosophy is reflected in the hiring policy. If two people are contending for a job, and one has 30 years experience and a distinguished record and the other has five years, but a great attitude, the five year person with the great attitude gets the job. Southwest knows most anyone can be trained to do nearly any job, but you can't be trained in values. Further, Southwest turns the organizational chart upside down, putting the front line workers at the top. These are the ones who make things happen by taking care of customers.

Boards of Advisors[16]

You are the CFO of a $12 million dollar privately held company. New entrants into the market are competing based on price, and their quality is improving. Your customers are loyal, but you know they won't say no to competitors' price incentives much longer. Your boss, the owner, is terrified. She knows new ideas are needed, but is terrified of asking outsiders to join the

---

[15] I highly recommend reading, *NUTS! Southwest Airlines' Crazy Recipe for Business and Personal Success,"* Kevin and Jackie Freiberg, Bard Press, 1996.

[16] Adapted from "Board of Directors vs. Board of Advisors," Gary D. Zeune, *The Financial Manager's Report*, AICPA, October 1995, p. 5.

board of directors — to ask outsiders to peer into the inner workings of the company — and give them voting power.

What about using consultants? Usually an expensive proposition, consultants normally don't stick around to see the real-life implications of their suggestions. And, consultants tend to push CEOs toward a solution that will utilize their area of expertise.

What's the solution? A board of *advisors*. John Nash, president of the National Association of Corporate Directors estimated that 80% of private company owners considering outside directors end up putting together a board of advisors. A more informal arrangement, a board of advisors has no voting power, so is less threatening, and, generally has no legal liability to protect shareholder interests.

Like a board of outside directors, the goal is to assemble a team of more experienced group of advisors. As a result, a certain amount of second-guessing will make your CEO uncomfortable. But, that pales in comparison to the uncertainty the rest of the company will feel. If not dealt with in a forthright manner, such stress can nearly cripple a company, at the very time it can least afford the distraction. Management will fear being second-guessed by more seasoned executives. Let the employees know up front that the board's mission is strategic;

advisors will not get involved in day-to-day operations. Also, keep the management team informed about the candidates. Ask employees how they would select advisory members, let appropriate management join the interviewing process. Familiarity significantly reduces the stress.

A board of advisors has other benefits. Many members will have been senior executives. If the relationship is handled properly, advisors will be there for the long haul. Advisors have no particular ax to grind and are also substantially less expensive than consultants. Don't expect your advisors to rubber-stamp decisions. Advisors will shake up the company culture by asking hard questions — questions that make you sweat and squirm in your seat. They will require a break with the old way of thinking.

> **Sacred cows make the best hamburger.**

What kind of people do you want on your board of advisors? Foremost, you need a fresh perspective. That means people who don't even know about your company. So how are you going to find them? Since the company is in crisis, you probably don't have the time or the expertise to find them. But, some executive recruiting firms specialize in finding advisors. Ask around for references.

You will likely be drawn to candidates who challenge. Prepare for the interviews by deciding what approach you are going to take -- the hard sell, or let the candidates form their own opinions by asking questions.

The most critical issue is why each candidate wants to be an advisor. If someone asks you to raise the meeting fee, they may be primarily interested in a second income. If an investment banking candidate continually talks about the firm's financing capability, the real issue may be earning a fee by taking the company public or raising private capital. Look for candidates who bombard you with enthusiastic questions about the company and offer ways they can help.

Sacred cows make the best hamburger. Expect the board to slay a lot of sacred cows. For example, many owners focus on the internal workings of the company and use this view to market the business. But, most customers don't care about the company's internal workings. They only care if you solve their problems. For example, say you run a technical training school for high school graduates. Students don't care about the equipment. Students are interested in getting a job. Instead of promoting your state-of-the-art equipment (an internal view), advisors might suggest a strategic shift in your marketing -- promote the number of job offers your graduates receive.

Once in place, how do you keep the board running smoothly? Some suggestions. At each meeting, schedule the next several meetings. Prepare name tents to force management to mingle with advisors. Begin and end meetings on time. Have a set agenda. Have lunch with at least one advisor between meetings. Keep the board's role strategic. As managers sort out which board ideas they want to implement, they will form natural bonds with the advisors to implement the plans. Managers losing power to advisors will transform into power to be used.

Properly formed and utilized, boards of advisors can be extremely valuable in changing the secretive culture found at most private companies. Why adopt a board of advisors? Because you can't afford not to. The world is changing much too fast to ignore the vast talent that is available for the asking. But if needed, you must make changes. Board members will not tolerate leaders who won't admit what they don't know.

Gary D. Zeune, CPA

Using over 20 years of experience in auditing, corporate finance, and investment banking, Gary D. Zeune, CPA, provides CPAs, attorneys and executives with hands-on experience in fraud, performance measurement, and capital acquisition. Mr. Zeune instructs courses for:

- FBI and US Attorney
- The SEC Institute
- National Association of Securities Dealers
- North American Securities Administrators Association
- American Society for Industrial Security
- Over 35 state CPA societies and bar associations
- American Institute of CPAs
- American Management Association
- Institute of Management Accountants
- Entrepreneurship Institute
- Treasury Management Association
- Private classes for numerous companies and accounting firms.

Mr. Zeune has instructed Strategy Formulation and Implementation in the Executive MBA Program and Accounting and Honors Finance at The Ohio State University. He is also a member of the Education Executive Council and is past chairman of the Education Marketing and Public Relations Committees of The Ohio Society of CPAs. His other memberships include: the American Institute of CPAs, and the Regulation of Public Offerings Committee of the Ohio Division of Securities.

Prior to forming his consulting practice in 1986, Mr. Zeune was an Assistant Vice President of Corporate Finance at The Ohio Company, a Columbus, Ohio investment banking firm. He also spent more than five years in Treasury and Finance at Wendy's International, where he was responsible for mergers and acquisitions, financial and SEC reporting, and corporate finance. He was on the audit staff of Ernst & Ernst from 1973 to 1977; and taught accounting at Ohio University from 1970 to 1973, where he received his bachelors in mathematics and master's in accounting, with honors.

Mr. Zeune is widely published. He is the author of *The CEO's Complete Guide to Committing Fraud, Outside the Box,* and the forthcoming *Going Public: What the CFO Needs to Know,* to be published by the American Institute of CPAs. He is a member of the Editorial Advisory Board of the *Journal of Working Capital Management* and *The Ohio CPA Journal.* For Deloitte & Touche, he authored *Financing Business Growth* and has completed the first draft of *The Complete Guide to*

Buying or Selling a Closely Held Business, two books in the firm's Entrepreneurial Series. He has authored chapters for two books published by Warren Gorham Lamont, the world's largest financial publisher: "Accessing the Capital Markets" and "Options for Raising Capital."

Mr. Zeune's magazine or journal articles include:
- *New Fraud Standards Change Auditor's Role*
- *SAS 82 Requires More of Auditors — And Boards*
- *Fraud: You and Your Customers Are Now in the Spotlight*
- *How to Fool Your Auditors*
- *Non-financial Performance Measures*
- *Initial Public Offerings: Red Herrings, Green Shoes and Blue Skies*
- *Using the Hidden Information in Accounts Receivable*
- *Initial Public Offerings*
- *Flawed Analysis: How Seasonality Inaccurately Alters Traditional Ratios*
- *Keeping Track of Your Cash, Are Your Ratios Adequate?*
- *Going Public: What You Need to Know*
- *Floating a Stock Offering: New Buoyancy from the SEC*
- *Ducks in a Row: Orchestrating the Flawless Public Stock Offering*

- *Small Business Rush to Capital Markets*
- *Board of Advisors vs. Board of Directors*
- *Why Financial Reporting Must Change*
- *Proposed Auditing Standard Would Set New Guidelines for Fraud Detection*